Paul Poiret.

H. Poiret

Elsa Schiaparelli

Christian Dior

pierre Balmain

Gabrielle Chanel

Yves Saint Laurent

COUTURE CONFESSIONS

COUTURE CONFESSIONS

FASHION LEGENDS IN THEIR OWN WORDS

Pamela Golbin

Illustrated by Yann Legendre

Mad Ellen and ChaCha Nelly have often invited me to tea, but I've always been stood up. The toiles and garments have spoken to me in hushed tones. Their messages whispered to me through ropes of pearls and mercurial cutting. Now with clarity, illuminated, they speak.

— John Galliano

The author gratefully acknowledges all primary sources researched during the preparation of this book and wishes to thank those writers, journalists, and historians whose interviews were used in support of this project.

Couture Confessions:
Fashion Legends in Their Own Words

First published in the United States of America in 2016 by
Ex Libris, an imprint of
Rizzoli International Publications, Inc.
300 Park Avenue South
New York, NY 10010
www.rizzoliusa.com

Publication © 2016 Pamela Golbin
Illustrations © 2016 Yann Legendre

Book design by Modern Activity
Translations from the French by Philippe Aronson

2016 2017 2018 2019 2020 / 10 9 8 7 6 5 4 3 2 1
ISBN: 978-0-8478-4903-1
Library of Congress Control Number: 2015952944

Printed in China

Despite thorough research, all attempts to trace the copyright holder of
Pierre Balmain's *My Years and Seasons*, last published by the Orion
Publishing Group, were unsuccessful. The publisher welcomes any
information on this title with regard to its copyright holder.

Grateful acknowledgment to the Victoria & Albert Museum for their
permission to excerpt text from *Shocking Life* by Elsa Schiaparelli, first
published by J.M. Dent & Sons Ltd., 1954. This edition first published by
the V&A Publications, 2007. V&A Publishing. Victoria & Albert
Museum, South Kensington, SW7 2RL. www.vandapublishing.com

CONTENTS

INTRODUCTION

PAMELA GOLBIN IN CONVERSATION
WITH HAMISH BOWLES

*Pamela, how did you first become excited by clothing—
and ultimately, by fashion?*

Like most people, I have an emotional connection to fashion. I first
visited a costume exhibition when I was about five or six, in Paris.
It was an eighteenth-century exhibition of dress and I was fascinated
by the large "pannier" dresses and how women could move about in
them. It all began with asking questions about the how, what, where,
and why, which blossomed into a career.

*What intrigued you about the idea of a Q&A
with legendary designers from the past?*

For the Madeleine Vionnet retrospective I curated in 2009, I assem-
bled a great deal of firsthand material. Her voice was so compelling
that for the exhibition catalogue, instead of interpreting what she had
said, I let her speak directly to the reader. Very quickly it metamor-
phosed into a made-to-measure, exclusive, posthumous "interview."

    The response was so positive. Readers felt a real connection
with her. I received letters addressed to Vionnet from people who,
after reading the interview, thought she was still alive. I guess they
missed the fact that she passed away in 1975! I realized this format
not only gave the couturier's historical context but also allowed readers
to better understand the person behind the designer.

*What do you think a designer's words tell
us that their work doesn't?*

It's a very different type of information. Hearing them speak creates
a dialogue, a conversation. What I wanted to share was not only the
designers' successes but also their challenges and, specifically, their
individual points of view, which remain incredibly relevant today.

What determined your choice of designers?

The first thing is that they had to be dead! And then that their
influence on fashion had to be iconic. Paul Poiret, being the first
fashion superstar, was a great start. He's one of the very few
Parisian-born designers, and so the perfect voice to begin the
narrative of this book.

From there, I continued through to the present day with
Alexander McQueen. Not only does each interview tell a compelling
personal story, it also describes the couturiers' individual creative
process, showing how each one of these icons has a very different
perspective and a distinct way of expressing it. With this collection
of interviews, you have an oral history of twentieth-century fashion
told through the words of the legends who created it.

This book, for me, was inspired by Cecil Beaton's
The Glass of Fashion. I wanted to give readers a better understanding
of the "heroes and heroines" of fashion.

Which is something that you feel Cecil Beaton did with
The Glass of Fashion *for his contemporaries?*

Yes, it wasn't about a strictly academic point of view but a "personal
record of fashion," an anthology of the designers that "triumphed
the ephemeral," as Beaton put it.

*Are there any other twentieth-century fashion or style memoirs
that you feel have conveyed the same suggestion of intimacy and
very personal insight into designers' processes and personalities?*

Diana Vreeland's *D.V.* You feel as if you are sitting beside her and she
is giving you a fashion master class.

Today fashion is brand oriented. I wanted to give the reader access into the private studio of each of these designers, to learn more about them and what makes them tick.

Whom have you found to be the most eloquent of the designers?

Literally, the most eloquent is Christian Dior because he wrote many books. Chanel was the most incisive. Paul Poiret was captivating. McQueen was the most accessible and forthright. Lanvin was of an older generation, but she was a landmark in her own right. Vionnet was a true purist in her approach and precise in her answers; Balenciaga's silence was remarkable, yet he clearly left an indelible mark.

Balmain was particularly refined in his interviews and in the many conferences on architecture he gave over the years. Whether in French or in English, he spoke persuasively about fashion. Madame Grès was more reserved in the way she expressed herself. Yves Saint Laurent's melancholy is palpable and so are his piercing and perceptive comments on haute couture, ready-to-wear, and being a couturier.

Were there any great revelations for you that made you recalibrate the way you think about a designer's oeuvre? For example, by understanding more about his or her technical process or thought process?

What's incredibly fascinating is to see how diverse they were in expressing their talents. Obviously, there are the designers who were self-taught, such as Balmain, Dior, Chanel, and Schiaparelli, and those who had been to school, such as Saint Laurent, or received technical training, like Vionnet or McQueen, but nevertheless they each found their personal way to problem-solve in an industry that has not stopped transforming itself since the late nineteenth century.

So, it was more about showcasing their individual character traits.

Did you find that for all these very different and eclectic approaches to craft, to the métier of creating clothes, there is a continuum, even across the century?

Absolutely. One thing is evident: their love of fashion. Even if the designers came from incredibly varied backgrounds, they expressed the same passion. No matter how difficult it was, they persevered. They all had issues with time management, if I can put it that way. Whether it's Poiret or Lanvin or McQueen, they all speak about the timing challenges they face to design their collections.

We can see from their narratives that most of the issues prevalent in contemporary fashion were present at the beginning of the twentieth century: Is fashion art? Are designers considered artists or artisans? What is elegance? What is the importance of Paris as fashion capital? How should copying or counterfeiting be dealt with? These questions continue to resonate today. They all speak a very contemporary language, even if they practiced their art over a hundred years ago.

While there are these continuums that thread through the century, do these pan-generational designers also tell us about the fundamental changes in fashion through the century?

Funny enough, there are not that many changes. Fashion is cyclical in its evolving styles, but there are always the same issues at stake: how to produce more or differently and continue to stay innovative; the balance between commercial and creative collections; the cultural differences between different clienteles, in particular the American and the French; how to continue providing the highest standards in the ateliers.

Why is Balenciaga the only designer who is represented through additional voices?

Quite simply because he never gave an interview during his career, except for the one he agreed to at the end of his life. I couldn't think of publishing this book without having Balenciaga in it, so I chose to have his peers speak about him.

It says a lot about how respected he was within the fashion community: he was considered one of the masters of them all, although essentially he let his clothes alone speak for him.

Schiaparelli, on the other hand, was very instructive in the way she approached fashion, always wanting to share the latest pointers with her clients and her readers. And like many of the other designers' tips in this book, her advice is very contemporary.

What would you say has been the great takeaway for you working on this project?

The wonderful sense of humor shared by the designers. I tried to convey that systematically in each of the interviews. And I loved reading about how they described each other. Poiret comments on Chanel who in turn shares her opinions on Yves Saint Laurent who then pays tribute to Christian Dior. And Dior, the natural diplomat, speaks highly of all his peers.

At the end of the book I brought the legends together for a round table discussion and asked them the perennial question, What is fashion? I hope the lively visions of these eleven individual journeys will engage and inspire.

Enjoy!

PAUL POIRET

Monsieur Poiret, the press calls you the "king of fashion."
How do you feel about that?

Among the many things I've been called over the years, none has
given me greater pleasure. No title is better suited to flatter a man's
spirit, because the king of fashion reigns over all peoples, over the
whole world, and over sovereigns themselves — for all are subject
to the tyranny of fashion. Fashion influences you and your decision-
making insidiously, and it is a doubly despotic dictator, since it
commands women, who in turn direct the actions of men.[1]

What is your contribution to the vocabulary of couture?

Some have been good enough to say that I exercised a powerful influence over my age, and inspired an entire generation. It would be presumptuous of me to agree, and I must say it makes me feel uncomfortable; though if memory serves, when I started out all color was absent from fashion.[2]

Could you elaborate on that, please?

The faintest of pinks, lilac, swooning mauve, light hydrangea blue, watery green, pastel yellow, and the barest beige — all that was pale, soft, and insipid was held in high esteem. So I decided to let a few wolves into the sheep's pen — reds, greens, violets, *bleu de France* that raised the voices of the rest.[3]

You started a fashion revolution in 1907 by eliminating the corset.

It was in the name of liberty that I proclaimed the fall of the corset and the advent of the brassiere, which has ruled the day ever since.[4] I waged war on the corset.[5] It was around this time that I made Directoire-era-inspired dresses with the high waistline just below the bust, and with a brassiere replacing the corset.[6]

Yet there was a drawback.

Yes, I freed the bust but shackled the legs. Women complained of no longer being able to walk or get into a carriage.[7]

Is it true that a coat launched your career?

It was to become the template of a whole series of designs. And it is not farfetched to say that there is still something of this model in coats made everywhere today. In any case, for years, it dominated and inspired *la mode*. I called it "Confucius." Every woman had one. It was the beginning of the Oriental influence in fashion, of which I made myself the apostle.[8]

*You are Parisian by birth, which makes you
a rarity among Paris fashion designers.*

I am a Parisian of Paris; I was born in its heart, on the rue des Deux Écus,
in the First Arrondissement, where my father was a cloth merchant. It was
a little narrow street that joined the rue du Louvre and the rue Berger.[9]

What kind of childhood did you have?

I am told that one of the first phrases I uttered was *cron papizi* — my way
of asking for *crayon et papier*, or a pencil and paper. Thus, my vocation
as a painter revealed itself before my vocation as a designer; but my earliest
efforts were not preserved — they seem to have held no interest or meaning
save for myself. I spent my days in my mother's apartment on the second
floor and in my father's shop, which I was sometimes allowed to visit.[10]

Were you already interested in fashion?

Did I already dream of stuffs and chiffons? I think I must have.
I was passionately drawn to women and their clothing; I combed
through catalogues and magazines searching for everything
pertaining to fashion; I was very much a dandy, and if I sometimes
forgot to wash, I never forgot to change my collar.[11]

How did your taste for fashion manifest itself?

At home in the evening I went to my room and dreamed up
sumptuous outfits. My sisters had presented me with a little wooden
mannequin forty centimeters high, and I pinned my silks and muslins
on it. What delightful evenings I owe to that doll, which I dressed
up first as a piquant Parisienne, and then as an Eastern queen.[12]

*What other memories of your childhood in the late
nineteenth century can you share with us?*

When I was a child my parents would take me to the Palais Royal.
I was irresistibly drawn to Flamand — the ice cream vendor on rue de
Valois: the extraordinarily rich color spectrum of the various sherbets
gave an impression of coolness I felt I could almost bathe in. Later
in life I felt the same emotion looking at organdy cloth.[13]

You seem to have had a rather wonderful childhood.

Precisely at seven o'clock my family sat down to dinner, and forty-five minutes later I was already at the Comédie Française, waiting for the doors to open. Then I would run up the stairs four at a time and choose the best of the cheapest seats.[14]

Your career had humble beginnings, did it not?

In the years when the great Exposition of 1889 was being prepared, we saw, every morning and evening, the progress of construction of the Eiffel Tower, and each of us had his comment to make. It was hard for me to complete my work at school, as there were so many different distractions calling me in all directions and I was impatient to taste all the joys of life. At eighteen I finished school and my father, whose greatest fear was that I should choose a career for myself, found me a job with one of his friends, an umbrella manufacturer. It was hard for me.[15]

Is that where you learned the tricks of the trade?

Naturally, I thought only of escaping that occupation. My job was delivering umbrellas to Bon Marché, to the Louvre, to Trois-Quartiers, crisscrossing Paris in my work coat, a heavy bundle of umbrellas on my shoulder. My boss wanted to kill my pride. Apparently he failed, for my pride is still intact all these years later.[16] I began to sketch outlandish outfits, outlined in India ink, always with inventive detail. One day, encouraged by a daring friend, I took some designs to Madame Chéruit, in the house she shared with the Raudnitz Soeurs. It worked: Madame Chéruit had me brought into her office from the dark passage where I was awaiting her opinion. I had never seen anything more disturbing than this lovely woman in the midst of so much elegance.[17]

And then a golden opportunity fell right into your lap.

One day in 1896 Monsieur Doucet suggested that instead of laying my eggs in every basket, I should produce designs for him alone. He offered to keep me with him and to buy all my designs. When I told my father he refused to believe me, so little knowledge had he of my calling, and so little confidence in my success.[18] That's how I became a designer. The Maison Doucet was then at the height of its prosperity . . . It was a blessed time, devoid of cares or worries and full of joie de vivre.[19]

How did your first meeting with Monsieur Doucet go?

As I listened to him, I thought that he was saying everything that I wanted to say, and that he was the man I wished to become. In my imagination, I was already the Doucet of the future. I did not want any other role model in life. I would have liked to make myself in his image.[20]

You were then suddenly thrust into an intriguing world. Can you tell us about it?

Monsieur Doucet said to me, "I am putting you in as one throws a dog into the water to teach him to swim. You must manage as best you can." And I managed.[21] My first design was a little red cloak with bands of cloth around the neckline. The lapels were formed by the gray crepe de chine lining, and it was fastened with six enamel buttons up one side. Four hundred were sold. Some clients wanted it in every color. My reputation was made. One day I saw, arriving in her mule-drawn carriage, the person who in my opinion embodied the genius, grace, and spirit of Paris: Réjane. She passed through the doorway with a great swishing of silk and asked for Monsieur Doucet, who immediately appeared, handsome as a god.[22]

Chez Doucet I saw all the stars of that time: Marthe Brandès, Theo, Mary Garden, Reichenberg. And I was delighted beyond measure when we were chosen to dress the yearly revue at the Épatant, on rue Boissy d'Anglas. One year, we dressed the corps de ballet of the Opéra as soldiers of the First Empire.[23]

Did you find it disconcerting to start out at a big fashion house?

I was very much at a loss when introduced to the vendeuses. They were for the most part aged, Old Guard harpies firmly ensconced at the house like mites in cheese. They had tremendous sway over their clientele, speaking familiarly to the great ladies, taking them by the waist to give them advice in condescending tones.[24]

Was the workload intense?

We created new designs each week. The belles of that day displayed them at the Sunday races, refusing ever to be seen in the same outfit twice. These ladies — Liane de Pougy, Émilienne d'Alençon, La Belle Otéro — were the darlings of the fashionable grand dukes and royalty.[25]

What are your fondest memories of that time?

I liked to stay in Doucet's salons on Saturday evening, when the Sunday deliveries were being prepared. It gave me extreme pleasure to look at and touch all the dresses that twenty-four hours later would be the talk of Paris. Then, on Sunday I would go to the races to admire the bearing of these high priestesses of elegance while dreaming up new, more astonishing, more striking designs.[26]

But eventually you left.

Not without reason. I designed some new outfits for my girlfriend, who could not afford clothes from the great houses. She took my designs to a seamstress, who made them for her. Monsieur Doucet learned of this, and that was one of his reasons for depriving himself of my services.[27]

Next, in 1901, you joined the venerable House of Worth.

At that time, the Maison Worth was directed by Jean and Gaston, the two sons of the great couturier who had once dressed the Empress Eugénie. Gaston said, "Young man, you know the Maison Worth. It possesses the richest, most exalted clientele, but today this clientele does not dress exclusively for state functions. Princesses sometimes travel by horse-drawn bus, and go on foot in the streets.

My brother Jean has always refused to make the simple
and practical dresses that are much in demand. We are like some
great restaurant that serves nothing but truffles. What we need now
is a potato fryer." I immediately saw what an opportunity it would
be for me to become this great house's potato fryer, so I didn't
hesitate to accept the offer.[28]

*You stayed there for just two years and opened
your own house in 1903.*

At 5 rue Auber, at the corner of the rue Scribe, there were premises
that had previously belonged to a tailor who had gone out of business.
That did not frighten me. I resolved to set up shop there. My father,
who might have attempted to dissuade me, had by this time passed
away. My mother, who saw in my eyes the fire that is the key to
success, loaned me fifty thousand francs.[29]

Were you an immediate success?

Within a month the house was famous. One day Réjane came
in her mule-drawn carriage. It was an event. She came back often.[30]

What a wonderful time in history.

It was on returning from a Bal des Quat'Z'Arts, in the month of
May 1911, I think, that I decided to throw an unforgettable fête
called "The Thousand and Second Night" in my salons and gardens
in Paris. I gathered together several artists and put my resources at
their disposal to create something that the world had never before
seen.[31] The wealthy artists and sensitive amateurs who attended the
gathering, such as Princess Murat and Monsieur Boni de Castellane,
said that never in their lives had they ever seen anything as thrilling
as the shows put on that miraculous night.

Some say that those fêtes were nothing more than self-
promotion, but I want to put a stop to that stupid insinuation: I am
not nor have I ever been a man who pays in order to be discussed.[32]

Around the same time, you also founded a school.

I gave the school of decorative art the name of one of my daughters, Martine.[33] My role in the school consisted of stimulating the pupils' activity and taste, without ever influencing or criticizing them, so that the source of their inspiration remained pure and intact. Truth be told, they had much more sway over me than I had over them, and my only talent consisted of choosing from all their work the items that were most suitable for production.[34]

How do you design your collection?

I don't want to talk about how wonderful my dresses are, for I hope their quality will speak for itself; however, I will say that they were created out of a desire for harmony. Their components are consistent in character. And this is because all those who have a hand in making my dresses — from the silk manufacturer who supplies the source material to the embroiderer who embellishes it — are in close contact with me. We pool our ideas together, sharing our tastes and lines of investigation through daily conversations and interaction. Certain silk manufacturers are free to come and go as they please in my house; they look at my collection, get a feeling for the things I need, and act accordingly. My embroiderers are present when a design comes into being. They sit next to the *premières* as they work, and intuit what the dress will need — whether the stitching should be bright or matte, for example. So I would say that every stage of production is character-ized by teamwork. Thus is consistency achieved: through compro-mise, mutual respect, and camaraderie — at least I hope so.

This is what I have attempted to accomplish, and if you say I have succeeded, I will be the happiest man alive.[35] To dress a woman is not to cover her with ornaments; it is to envelop nature in a signifi-cant contour which accentuates her grace. All the talent of the artist consists in the manner of revealment.[36]

Do you instinctively recognize when a design is finished?

I feel satisfied with my creations only if they give an impression of simple charm, of the calm perfection comparable to what one feels when standing before an antique statue. I find my gowns satisfying only when all the details of which they are composed disappear into the general harmony of the whole.[37]

How do you feel about the word "artist"?

While making my dresses, I feel that they are works of art: I project something of my personality in the material. When I choose a pleat it is more than a pleat — it is a creative path, and from that path springs the line, the style.[38] The designer must abandon all sense of self-importance. Adored by women, he is hated by men, and therefore finds himself at a kind of crossroads; he is a hybrid being whose contact with the public is always influenced by this dual point of view. If he is intelligent, which sometimes is the case, he will enjoy the positive cultural benefits of his position and not let the contempt of the male population get him down.[39]

Designers decide what is in fashion, don't they?

Do you believe that? You don't seem to be very knowledgeable about how things work . . . What godforsaken village do you come from? Women decide what is in fashion . . . the all-powerful religion for which we are merely the priests . . . We do everything to please our clientele, but we cannot be responsible for their verdicts . . . I create two hundred designs each season, offering women two hundred different ideas. Is it my fault if they always choose the same dress?[40] As a designer and innovator, I only have extremely unambiguous things to say!

The avant-garde designer — such as myself — has to have his wits about him. He must be tenacious and farsighted. It's not always easy! The greatest obstacle to bringing his ideas to light is the fact that he has to share his work with those who produce — and often destroy — it.[41]

Any thoughts on your colleagues? I'd be particularly curious to hear what you have to say about the person you called "the pioneer of the industry of la grande couture,"[42] *Charles Frederick Worth?*

Draped in plush capes, haughty and self-assured, his fat moustache drooping from his upper lip, a velour beret nonchalantly hanging over one ear, Monsieur Worth would strike poses in front of the mirrors in his salons on rue de la Paix. He was the first to proclaim himself an "artist couturier."[43] He was an extremely audacious man, but his taste — which made his son Jean's cheeks flush on more than one occasion — was often rather poor. His avowed weakness for the pompous, the baroque, and the rococo prevent him today from being considered a master. Yet he will be remembered for having foreseen, created, and implemented the immense development of the couture industry.[44]

Anyone else worthy of mention?

Jacques Doucet's parents, who owned a lingerie shop, set him up at 21 rue de la Paix. Monsieur Jacques, who would become my most revered mentor, was then a very elegant young fellow whose charm and knowledge made him a very popular man about town.[45]

What about your contemporaries,
Coco Chanel and Jean Patou?

Honestly, I don't see what Chanel or Patou brought or added to the profession, though I admit they both have a good eye and are very skillful at widely disseminating the innovations of their colleagues.[46]

You have quite a reputation, don't you?

My detractors have often harped on a warning that I had painted on the door of my office that read, "DANGER! Before knocking, ask yourself three times: Is it of utmost importance to disturb HIM?". And yet this straightforward warning did little to protect me from unwelcome visitors. Designers often acquire a reputation for insolence. Women like that, even though they tend to deny it. The more a designer is outrageous and extravagant, the more he amuses and intrigues women. Once he is successful, his personality attracts imitators and inspires coquettish behavior. People are always doing cartwheels to get his attention. He lets himself enjoy the rather facile fruits of his success, rumors start swirling around him, and soon his reputation is made: he is a character, a phenomenon, a superman, a genius.[47]

You don't mean to say that you treated your clients that way?

Depending on the case, I might be implacable and say, "Madame, you came to Poiret knowing that Poiret is the top house in the world. Very well then, I, Poiret, am telling you: this dress is good, it is beautiful, and it suits you. If you don't like it, too bad; send it away — but I will never make you another. We are not made to understand each other."[48]

I take it you feel quite strongly about the subject of copying.

I personally have been copied about as much as one can be, and I know both how difficult suppression is, and how little it accomplishes. I am almost tempted simply to let the counterfeiters do what they want, though I am in full agreement with *Le Moniteur*, and with Lucien Klotz, who wrote in *Le Matin* that a union should be set up to protect the victims of these misdeeds; the first order of business of such an organization would naturally be to convince lawmakers that what has heretofore been considered a mere peccadillo is, in fact, a crime. Madeleine Vionnet referred to them as thieves, and she was absolutely right; I don't see the gentleman who steals an idea out of my pocket as a competitor; he is a crook.[49]

Is a dress considered a work of art?

That a dress should be seen as a work of art is no longer in question, and like any work of art, it should be protected by law.[50] We shouldn't allow criticism to interfere with business: we are both artists and businessmen. Without getting angry, if I felt I was misunderstood I would reserve the right to defend my idea. The artist has the right of reply. It is up to me to decide if I need to use it. However, I do not fear the critics. I fear the day when nobody will talk about me anymore.[51]

Is being copied problematic for a designer?

The worst thing that can happen to a designer is *not* to be copied. For fashion means one thing: disseminating a successful idea. And if the idea spreads, it is not because of the designer, but because of the public's appreciation of it.[52]

How do you see the state of contemporary fashion?

I am convinced that the old fortress is crumbling. Times have changed.[53] Will today's fashion be relevant tomorrow?[54] Fashion needs a new master. He will have to do what I did: not look behind him, and consider nothing except what makes women beautiful.[55]

Are there certain rules that should be followed?

The art of dressing is an art as complex and elusive as all the others. It, too, has its principles and traditions, known only to persons of taste because they are in touch with their innermost feelings. This art has little to do with money.[56]

Could you be more precise?

The woman with limited resources has no more cause for being dowdily dressed than the rich woman has reason to believe she is beautifully clad. The contrary is very often true. Whereas the rich woman can satisfy her every whim in a most haphazard fashion, the woman of average means, simply because she is actually forced to *think* about her wardrobe, is more apt to realize what suits her and what doesn't. She learns how to choose and what to select. She acquires the art of dressing well.[57]

Are there fashions you do not appreciate?

Yes, I am against short skirts. On entering the reception room in my establishment, I see my many clients seated against the wall. It is nothing but an exhibition of legs. A sad sight! Short skirts — hmmm! The most mild thing I can say about them is that they are unbecoming.[58]

Are there other forms of art besides fashion that interest you?

Cinema must now set the tone and be to fashion what theater was twenty years ago, when opening nights were couture events. As long as the actors are dressed not by those who follow fashion but by those who create it, the silver screen will have a tremendous influence on contemporary taste. Otherwise, films with quite ordinary or even out of date costumes will become the norm.[59]

And how does one adapt fashion to the cinema?

It would perhaps be wiser to rephrase the question, for I believe
it is the cinema that must adapt to fashion.[60]

What challenges does that present?

In couture, much as in art, there are four important elements:
color, material, line, volume. Concerning cinema, color has to be left
aside momentarily. The material remains important. It would be a big
mistake to believe that material is unimportant in cinema. Today's
public knows how to "read" a photograph: not only the nature of
fabrics, but their weight, their flexibility, their texture — all of this
is perfectly expressed in photographs. The line remains important.[61]

How would you define happiness?

Happiness? To elevate oneself. Morally speaking, of course. Through art, philosophical ambition, knowledge. Happiness resides in moral peace and firmness. It is the sense of feeling one is leading a good, just, fair . . . and balanced life. When most people of a certain class think of happiness, they imagine pleasure. And the thing that characterizes our era is that we are submerged in pleasure — ha! — rather than happiness.[62]

In 1912 you were the first to take your dresses and models abroad.

I was the most popular designer in Paris, but I wanted the attention of the whole world. I decided to tour the major capitals of Europe with nine models. I don't know if I would have the strength today for such an arduous undertaking. For not only did I have to take nine models on a world tour — I was also responsible for bringing them all back to Paris safe and sound. I didn't want to come across as Barnum carting around prodigies, or a music-hall impresario. My tour had to maintain an air of distinction, and my advertising depended upon the good manners and behavior of these young ladies.[63]

Tell us about your models.

Well, one does not become a model on a whim; as for me, despite numerous requests, I do not entrust the work of showing off my dresses to women who don't know what they are doing. Society ladies? Impossible to work with. First of all, they quickly tire of the milieu; secondly, since they are used to wearing pretty dresses in their own manner, they are incapable of adopting a professional style. It's true, and this is no doubt a sign of the times, that the modeling profession now attracts many women who in the past would have looked down their noses at it. In general, six months of practice are necessary to become a model: you must learn to move, to walk, and to do all of that with elegance, and finesse — though the main challenge is to learn how to wear a coat and a dress with a plunging neckline.[64]

Could you tell us more about your trips —
to the United States for example?

First of all, I would like to point out that I was the first Parisian couturier to visit America. This will astonish nobody. I did not know exactly what I was going to do there, but I desired to make the acquaintance of that nation, which seemed so full of vitality and derring-do. I left one October morning.[65] I brought with me a film of my models in short dresses in my garden. When we arrived, before stepping ashore I was swarmed by an army of photographers and journalists who assailed me like mosquitoes. Never before had I encountered such curiosity and brashness.[66]

Everywhere you go, you are asked the same question:
What's next in fashion? I can't help but ask it as well.

I cannot answer your question. For the moment let us just consider what is.[67]

And yet, you must surely have thoughts on the matter.

Whenever I go to the United States, reporters ask me about tomorrow's fashion. If I say, "Skirts will remain short," on my return there is a delegation of cloth merchants awaiting me, to protest; if I say, "Skirts will get longer," I have a delegation from the hosiery industry; if I say, "Corsets are on their way out," the corset makers are in an uproar; if I say, "Turbans will be in vogue," the hairdressers complain. And yet, by definition fashion implies change. It favors each profession in turn.[68] There has never been a fashion that didn't, to paraphrase Beaumarchais, raise a hue and cry — a universal chorus of disapproval and disgust. Every new trend inspires suspicion and revulsion. The spirit of habit becomes indignant, and rebels in the name of custom and tradition. Have you dusted off the past? You find yourself accused of disavowing the glorious heritage of the fatherland — as if immoderation and whimsy weren't themselves French institutions.[69]

Could you explain how fashion is born?

In the old days, during the Second Empire for example, fashions were launched from on high, by the Empress Eugénie, or the Prince of Sagan. All the aristocracy would then immediately begin wearing the same dress, or jacket, or necktie. These days, it's the opposite. The movement starts in the lower echelons and moves upward. Sartorial fads are started by the midinettes, by members of the demimonde. The art of the couturier is knowing how to come up with something stylish and unique while embracing the inventive elements of these trends and leaving aside those aspects he finds aesthetically displeasing.[70]

*From an outsider's perspective, it appears difficult
to keep up with changes in fashion.*

One often hears complaints about anarchy in fashion; the journalists who go to the racetrack notice a thousand different directions and trends, but cannot make heads or tails of them. Why not return to one unique style? For example, in the seventeenth and eighteenth centuries all women dressed alike. Why not go back to that? The couturiers would love it. And the dresses from the time of Louis XIV and Louis XV would no doubt catch on quickly — if only women had not rejected corsets once and for all.[71]

*And yet, each season thousands of women ask the same
question: What will we be wearing this year?*

I can hardly repress a shrug when I hear someone ask, "What is going to be worn this year?" For the love of God, I say, Madame, choose for yourself the form and color of your clothes, and if someone tells you red will be in fashion, dare to wear violet; wear only what suits you, for there is only one principle of elegance and it is condensed in a word used by the Romans, *decorum*, meaning that which fits![72]

How would you define luxury?

There are but few people who do not mistake luxury for prettiness, costliness for elegance. Have you ever met a woman of means who did not own a string of pearls? Status is what they have first and foremost in mind. They wear their pearl necklaces to advertise their wealth, not to be more elegant or to show off dazzling skin; they don't wear them to be beautiful.[73]

You see at the opera hundreds of women who look like shrines. The flashiest women are never the most attractive. Quite the opposite. They are as aesthetically pleasing as a jeweler's tray; women who adorn themselves thusly, for the sake of displaying their fortune, might as well put their hair up in bank notes.[74]

The true *élégantes* are those who discover fashions, who dare, create — not those who follow.[75] There are in Paris at the present time only ten entities, ten silhouettes — no more; that is to say ten categories under which nearly all women are to be ranked. The ones who escape this classification are, in my opinion, the only *élégantes* worthy of the name.[76]

How do you feel about American women?

The American woman is the most independent in the world — the freest from tradition and convention.[77] It is she who should go farthest in the caprices and eccentricities of the mode. Let her dare to be different.[78]

Do you find them elegant?

Despite being rich and independent, American women dress like boarding-school girls. They are pretty, healthy, well-balanced, fulfilled, sporty, and they often have the natural type that is the closest to the Greek ideal, the perfection of architectural femininity . . . but one thing is missing: personality![79] Let her search for individuality, and, having found it, develop it in infinite modulations; then things most extravagant, most extraordinary and unexpected will be permitted her, for her role is to be seductive, to give pleasure, and to enliven the life of man.[80]

And Parisian women?

La Parisienne has always known how to adorn herself becomingly, having naturally the taste in keeping with their surroundings, with the class to which she belongs.[81]

What is it about the Parisian woman that is so appealing?

It is because of her ability to understand the eternal fitness of things that the *Parisienne* is so often the queen of large social functions![82]

What is the major difference between the two?

A *Parisienne*, especially, never adopts a design without making changes of capital importance to it and customizing it to suit herself. An American woman chooses the model presented to her and buys it just as it is, while a *Parisienne* wants it to be blue if it is green, or garnet if it is blue, and adds a fur collar, and changes the sleeves, and removes the bottom buttons.[83]

Do your clients receive guidance when they are choosing clothes?

At the moment when a woman chooses or orders a dress, she believes she is doing it in all freedom, in the full exercise of her own personality, but she is deceiving herself. It is the spirit of fashion that inspires her, that reigns over her intelligence and clouds her judgment.

Naturally, she defends herself against it. As you are listening to me speaking, the majority of you are thinking, "He is exaggerating. We are not the slaves of fashion to that extent, and we know how to dispense with following it when it does not please us." But here is where its miracle, its tour de force, resides: it always pleases, and its despotism is seductive by definition. Women are always of the same opinion as fashion, which changes its opinion continually.[84]

So, fashion has the last word?

Fashion? Fashion doesn't exist anymore! Look at the prints of yester-year. Every adjustment was minutely and inflexibly rendered. Now we have infinite variety, impulsiveness, individual tastes. Fashion today is what people like. The dress of today, the coat of tomorrow, are the dress and the coat that will best match the movements, face, and body of the woman who will wear them, or simply suit her desires. The couturier proposes; the woman disposes.[85]

What is your favorite style?

It depends. Each woman should flaunt her own unique flair, but my main concerns are color and light.[86]

Are there any guidelines you could share with us?

1 — Choose whatever is most becoming to your beauty.
2 — Choose the colors which go well with your complexion, your hair, your eyes.
3 — Observe the decorum and wear appropriate dresses in appropriate places.[87]

What are your founding principles?

I would say that they consist of two important points: the search for the greatest simplicity, and the taste for an original detail and personality.[88]

Do you have a favorite design?

I like a plain gown, cut from a light and flexible fabric, that falls from the shoulders to the feet in long, straight folds, like thick liquid, just touching the outline of the figure and throwing shadow and light over the moving form.[89]

You are known for your rather flamboyant dresses.

No matter how extravagant a design is, if it is simple, the dress will be beautiful.[90] And I maintain that the vivid colors and bizarre effects of Oriental fashions develop feminine beauty.[91]

Did you have a hard time with professional buyers?

It is more difficult than one thinks to make something new that is pretty, that fits, and that people like. And you know what? One always exaggerates beforehand the importance of the opinion that the buyers will have of our designs. We try very hard to innovate, to please them. And we're wrong. I strongly believe that the buyers go to work with an idée fixe, with preconceived notions; they only want to buy the models that most resemble those that were popular last season. They slow everything down by constantly clinging to the past, whereas what they should be doing is fighting for the future.[92]

Your maison *closed in 1929.*

I went from sheaths and dalmatics to flowers and bells. I infused them all with form, color, movement, life. I was respected, successful, world famous. It was too much. The bankers came along and they wanted to channel all of that; they took over my activities, thinking they could master them; and so it became like a doctor trying to heal a healthy man by force: he collapses his lungs in order to diagnose a collapsed lung, thus asserting the superiority of machine over man.[93]

Did fashion bring you happiness?

Fashion is of divine essence. I have no time for people who do not like fashion. As for me, I saw the writing on the wall. I was out of touch: I could no longer stand the fashion of my time, so I was bound to disappear.[94]

Any last words you would care to share with our readers?

I have no rancor at all. I have gotten used to the fact that I am no longer rich. Which is more than I can say for my taxman.[95]

⸂ NOTES ⸃

1   Paul Poiret, *En habillant l'époque* (Paris: Éditions Grasset, 1930), 272–73.

2   Poiret, *En habillant l'époque*, 77.

3   Poiret, *En habillant l'époque*, 77.

4   Poiret, *En habillant l'époque*, 63.

5   Poiret, *En habillant l'époque*, 62–63.

6   "La Mode Qui Vient! Quelques opinions de grands Couturiers," *L'Illustration*, June 11, 1921, 9.

7   Poiret, *En habillant l'époque*, 63.

8   Poiret, *En habillant l'époque*, 62.

9   Poiret, *En habillant l'époque*, 7.

10   Poiret, *En habillant l'époque*, 6–7.

11   Poiret, *En habillant l'époque*, 16.

12   Poiret, *En habillant l'époque*, 23.

13   Huguette Garnier, "Ce que sera la mode de l'été qui vient," *Excelsior*, April 12, 1923.

14   Poiret, *En habillant l'époque*, 17–18.

15   Poiret, *En habillant l'époque*, 21–22.

16   Poiret, *En habillant l'époque*, 22–23.

17   Poiret, *En habillant l'époque*, 23–24.

18 Poiret, *En habillant l'époque,* 25.

19 Poiret, *En habillant l'époque,* 28.

20 Poiret, *En habillant l'époque,* 26.

21 Poiret, *En habillant l'époque,* 31.

22 Poiret, *En habillant l'époque,* 31–32.

23 Poiret, *En habillant l'époque,* 33.

24 Poiret, *En habillant l'époque,* 29.

25 Poiret, *En habillant l'époque,* 36.

26 Poiret, *En habillant l'époque,* 37.

27 Poiret, *En habillant l'époque,* 45.

28 Poiret, *En habillant l'époque,* 53–54.

29 Poiret, *En habillant l'époque,* 60.

30 Poiret, *En habillant l'époque,* 62.

31 Poiret, *En habillant l'époque,* 171.

32 Poiret, *En habillant l'époque,* 177–78.

33 Poiret, *En habillant l'époque,* 146.

34 Poiret, *En habillant l'époque,* 148.

35 Paul Poiret, "Une conférence de Paul Poiret au Salon d'Automne," *L'Art et la Mode,* December 16, 1922.

36 Paul Poiret, "Poiret on the Philosophy of Dress," *Vogue,* October 15, 1913, 41.

37 Poiret, "Poiret on the Philosophy of Dress," 41.

38 Huguette, "La robe 'Oeuvre d'art' peut-être critiquée," *Excelsior,* April 15, 1924.

39 Paul Poiret, *Revenez-y* (Paris: Gallimard, 1932), 106.

40 Paul Poiret, "La Mode et la Mort," *Les Arts Décoratifs Modernes,* 1925.

41 Paul Poiret, "Quelques considérations sur la mode," *Le Figaro Artistique,* February 7, 1924.

42 Poiret, *En habillant l'époque,* 135–136.

43 Poiret, *Revenez-y,* 90.

44 Poiret, *Revenez-y,* 91.

45 Poiret, *Revenez-y,* 91.

46 Poiret, *Revenez-y,* 97.

47 Poiret, *Revenez-y,* 104–05.

48 Poiret, *En habillant l'époque,* 133–34.

49 *Moniteur de l'Exportation,* October 1920, 9.

50 "De la contrefaçon dans la couture," *Excelsior,* December 16, 1921.

51 Huguette, "La robe 'Oeuvre d'art' peut-être critiquée."

52 Marcel Zahar, "Faut-il poursuivre ou exploiter la copie," *Vu,* April 5, 1933, 511.

53 Zahar, "Faut-il poursuivre ou exploiter la copie."

54 H.G.N., "Comment se lance une mode — ce que nous dit M. Paul Poiret," *En attendant,* February 1923.

55 Poiret, *En habillant l'époque,* 78.

56 Paul Poiret, "Individuality in Dress," *Harper's Bazaar,* September 1912, 451.

57 Poiret, "Individuality in Dress," 451.

58 "Paul Poiret," *Harper's Bazaar,* August 1925.

59 Emma Cabire, "Le Cinéma & la Mode," *La Revue du Cinéma,* September 1, 1931, 32.

60 Cabire, "Le Cinéma & la Mode," 32.

61 Cabire, "Le Cinéma & la Mode," 32.

62 André Arnyvelde, "Le visage du Bonheur," *Paris Soir*, January 30, 1924.

63 Poiret, *En habillant l'époque*, 103.

64 *Excelsior*, November 22, 1922.

65 Poiret, *En habillant l'époque*, 236.

66 Poiret, *En habillant l'époque*, 237.

67 *En attendant*, February 1923.

68 "La Mode," *Information Sociale*, October 26, 1922.

69 Paul Poiret, "Paul Poiret, Défense de la Mode," *La Revue Rhénane*, 718.

70 *En attendant*, February 1923.

71 Geraldine, *Les Dessous Élégants*, May 1921, 60.

72 "Ideals of Elegance in Dress," *Vogue*, July 8, 1909. This text has been edited from the original English, which read, "I can hardly repress a shrug of the shoulders when I hear someone asking, What is going to be worn this year? For the love of the Bon Dieu, I say, Madame, choose yourself the form and color of your clothes, and if one tells you red will be much worn dare to wear violet restrict you choice to wear what suits you, for there is only one principle of elegance and it is condensed in a word used by the Romans, "decorum"; that means the thing that suits!"

73 "Ideals of Elegance in Dress." This text has been edited from the original English, which read, "There are but few people who do not confound what is luxurious with what is pretty, what is costly with what is elegant. Have you met a single woman having a sufficient income who does not adorn herself. It has come to express a kind of pompous formula of position. They put on their collars of pearls to advertise, not for the sake of to be more elegant, or for the sole purpose of setting off the brilliancy of their, of adding to their beauty.

74 "Ideals of Elegance in Dress." This text has been edited from the original English, which read, "You see at the opera hundreds of women adorned like shrines. The most dazzling and sumptuous are never the most seducing. Very much the contrary Quite the opposite. One experiences in contemplating them no more aesthetic emotion than before a jeweler's tray, and women who adorn themselves in this way, for the sake of displaying their fortune, seem to me less beautiful than if they put their hair up in bank notes.

75 "Ideals of Elegance in Dress."

76 "Ideals of Elegance in Dress."

77 Poiret, "Poiret on the Philosophy of Dress," 41.

78 Poiret, "Poiret on the Philosophy of Dress," 41.

79 Marie-Thérèse Cuny, "Le look Poiret," *Jours de France*, November 1984, 18.

80 Poiret, "Poiret on the Philosophy of Dress."

81 "Ideals of Elegance in Dress," 36.

82 "The Ten Commandments of Paul Poiret," *Harper's Bazaar*, October 1912, 521.

83 Poiret, En habillant l'époque, 134.

84 Poiret, *En habillant l'époque*, 273.

85 "Dans le Royaume de la Mode," *Crapouillot*, April 1, 1921.

86 "Nos Interviews," *Le Matin*, June 7, 1923.

87 "The Ten Commandments of Paul Poiret," 521.

88 Poiret, "Poiret on the Philosophy of Dress."

89 Poiret, "Poiret on the Philosophy of Dress."
    This text has been edited from the original
    English, which read, "I like a plain gown,
    cut from a light and supple fabric, which
    falls from the shoulders to the feet in long,
    straight folds, like thick liquid, just
    touching the outline of the figure and
    throwing shadow and light over the
    moving form."

90 Poiret, "Poiret on the Philosophy of Dress."
    This text has been edited from the original
    English, which read, "One may wear the
    most extravagant, the most fantastic of
    robes; No matter how extravagant a design
    is, if the design is simple, the gown will
    be beautiful."

91 "How Poiret Conducts an Opening,"
    Vogue, April 15, 1912, 36. This text has been
    edited from the original English, which
    read, "I maintain that the straight, clinging
    line is the line of beauty, that the vivid
    colors and bizarre effects of oriental modes
    develop feminine beauty, and on these
    points I cannot change my mind."

92 "Dans la Couture, Un interview de Paul
    Poiret," *L'Officiel de la couture et de la mode*,
    no. 2, 1921, 13.

93 Paul Poiret, "En habillant l'époque,"
    Éditions Grasset, Paris, 1930, 303.

94 Paul Poiret, "Paul Poiret, Les divines
    aberrations de la mode," *Vogue* (France),
    January 1938, 39.

95 Cuny, "Le look Poiret," 18.

JEANNE LANVIN

Madame Lanvin, thank you for agreeing to this interview.

You have come to ask me the relation of dressmaking to art, is it not so?[1]

Absolutely, but we are also interested in your feelings about the profession that you have been practicing without interruption since 1885 — a long career that makes you the doyenne of fashion.

To me, of course, it seems one of the greatest of the arts, for I am sure that one must have more than a "flair" for dress designing if one would create beautiful frocks. One must have real talent for this, just as much as for painting, music, sculpture, or architecture. It is not something which can be acquired. It is a gift, but like all those other gifts it must be cultivated.[2]

Do you see parallels between dressmaking and other art forms?

I build my clothes much as a sculptor works on the figure, molding
the lines to it, for I look upon dress designing as akin to sculpture.[3]

What makes haute couture different from the other arts?

Dressmaking is a fascinating art. It is preeminently French and
therefore dear to the hearts of all French people. It is an art based
on history, and like history, it is ever changing.[4]

Could you be more precise?

Couture is not an abstract art. One designs a type of dress for a type
of woman, and the beauty of fashion is inspired by fashionable beauty.[5]

So, do you see the designer as an artist?

We are creators first and foremost! And our only concern
must be to make ever more beautiful dresses.[6]

Does contemporary fashion continue to surprise you?

Never before has fashion been more dependent upon the
charm of the woman. Everything hinges on her lithe body.[7]

What is fashion to you?

Fashion is — don't you agree? — an art of infinite variety
that seldom reaches in to the part of inspiration.[8]

How do you see the female silhouette evolving?

The styles change slowly nowadays, and every new gown I present
suggests the bigger change of subsequent ones. Every slight change
is part of a considerable change.[9]

What is your favorite kind of dress?

I love designing a romantic dress. I suppose I have designed
thousands of them, but I am never tired of it.[10]

*You are known for robes de style that you yourself
define as "a clinging bodice rising above a billowing
skirt of rich or dainty fabric."[11]*

It is true that the robe-de-style is by far my favorite type of creation,
and that the curtains have never parted once upon one of my
collections in which many such gowns have not been included.[12]
I am sure that two thousand years from now, when archaeologists
reconstruct the remains of what we now call modern civilization,
there will be only one "typical" costume for women, which will
be found to have appeared again and again. . . That is the tight
bodiced, full skirted, floor-length gown that we in the twentieth
century call the robe-de-style.[13]

How do you start designing a dress?

I always begin by leaving things out.[14]

So what is the next step?

I work in my own way. I never draw a dress beforehand for I am
never sure what I am going to do . . . I have my material and a *première*
to follow my instructions in arranging the one on the other. I know
nothing of the technicalities of dressmaking. It would be impossible
for me to make a frock with my own hands, but I know instinctively
when a line is wrong or the colors do not harmonize or when the
effect is not chic.[15]

Do you design the entire collection yourself?

Indeed, for thus only does a house have personality. . . I design
not only the models for frocks and coats but also for lingerie
and furs and jewelry.[16] You are aware of the immense amount
of work, research, and expense that go into creating a new
collection. This effort, that we have to replicate at least four
times a year, makes demands on us, our collaborators, and our
seamstresses — an incessant daily labor whose moral and material
price you can surely guess.[17]

Is that why you are so involved in the fight against copying?

It is only natural that a successful design be *imitated*. Imitation
does not bother me. It is normal, inevitable, flattering even
— not to mention useful, since it constantly forces us designers
to come up with new ideas. . . But if by *copy* you mean what I mean
— that is to say an out and out forgery, a perfect replica of all or
part of our designs — that is unacceptable. We are no longer talking
about imitation or inspiration, but theft.[18]

How important is femininity in fashion?

I believe every woman's clothes should emphasize her feminine charm.[19] I am in favor, first of all, of greater femininity in women's dress so far as it is compatible with the changed conditions of modern life, and I am doing everything in my power to bring about its return.[20] Women have come back to realize that their greatest asset is their feminine charm. Even your businesswomen no longer find it necessary to dress in severe masculine dress. They have discovered that soft beautiful feminine things, restrained of course, and simple in their line, are a real asset in business.[21]

Is elegance simply the expression of femininity?

Of course, the great factor in dress elegance is personality; and no matter how much personality a woman may have, it will be repressed if she does not feel comfortable, physically and mentally.[22]

The simplification of the contemporary wardrobe was a major change in fashion.

Of course, I realize that conditions of today do not permit a complete return to the elegance of yesteryear — the woman who goes in for sports, the woman who drives her own car, the woman who has a profession, can not load herself down with garments impractical for those things. We are commencing to bring back gracefulness and soft beauty wherever possible... We realize that just because a woman drives her own car during the daytime, or plays tennis in the morning, dressed suitably, is no reason why the same woman need dress with the same Spartan simplicity in the evening, at dinner or the theater.[23]

How do you feel about young women's clothes today?

Instead of being themselves, and enjoying a privilege that swiftly fades, young girls have a tendency to dress like older women. And unfortunately they end up looking exactly like their mothers. As for me, I try to teach them that they need have only two dresses instead of ten, as long as they have been chosen by a sure and competent hand.[24]

What advice would you give young women today?

Their femininity is their most priceless gift, it is unique.[25]

Are there materials you use that emphasize youth?

Silver and gold lamé, apart from their stateliness and practical advantages, make women look young; and an important step toward making a woman look elegant is to make her look young: not because age cannot be elegant as well as youth — far be it from the truth — but because a woman looks more elegant when she feels self-confident and self-contained.[26]

When a woman finds choosing a design difficult,
what questions should she ask herself?

A woman should ask herself if a certain dress looks like herself and accordingly accept, or reject it. . . She too often, alas, selects a thing because the Duchess So-and-So or the grand and rich Mrs. So-and-So has one like it, and not because she herself requires it as a supplement to her own personality.[27]

What are your thoughts on Parisian women?

The *Parisienne* is a woman who has a feeling for nuance and measure; a woman who knows to choose shoelaces that match her dress.[28]

You seem to have a special appreciation for American women. Why?

These American women — they are wonderful. Their figures, it is marvelous how they preserve them. There are no old women in the United States. They are all young. And they wear their clothes better than any women in the world.[29]

Could you tell us where you find your sources of inspiration?

In everything and from everywhere. . . I travel a great deal and I read, read, read. I often get an idea from a ponderous old volume of history or geography. Ideas come to me from extraordinary sources, but they must be developed always within these four walls.[30]

Is it correct to say that Paris is the epicenter of your activity?

I do my best work in Paris. I may find inspiration in the frieze of a temple in ancient Greece or in a Velázquez portrait in the Prado Gallery in Madrid, but try as I may, I cannot work out my idea until I am back here. Here only, in my little corner among my books and documents, am I able to put my ideas into form.[31]

Do you believe that couturiers can do without the City of Light?

We do not impose the *mode* — we try to sense it. I like to say that the *mode* is the air of Paris. Take the best of Parisian designers, shut him up away from contact with the outside world, or send him away to some foreign country — he will be worth nothing.[32]

Have you been influenced by cinema?

By putting modern women on the screen, cinema has definitely had a considerable influence on me, renewing and enriching my inspiration. . . Also, cinema is an international art form, and the type of woman that it displays is also international. By introducing us to foreign beauties, the cinema has enriched and amplified our inspiration. And this state of affairs has not been detrimental to Paris — on the contrary: its power as the capital of taste has only spread further, and been felt by women from countries all over the world.

Thanks to the big screen, the feminine ideal has been renewed, making it ever more beautiful and harmonious, and nearer to the perfection of antiquity, while retaining its essential mystery.[33]

What is the biggest difference between fashion and cinema?

Cinema tends to amplify things . . . That is why I exaggerate a style in order to accentuate the character as much as possible when I am working on a film.[34]

The Lanvin house remained open during the war years.
It must have been a particularly arduous time.

Life goes on, no matter how hard things may get. And it is a woman's duty to remain as elegant as possible. Think of all those whose living depends upon feminine elegance . . . and everything that goes along with it! Naturally, balance is required. With discretion and distinction as its watchwords, couture was able to set the tone.[35]

What were your priorities at the time?

Innovation is intimately linked to the difficult problem of transportation. How and why should we change the feminine silhouette, as long as we remain dependent on the bicycle and the subway! Wartime restrictions forced fashion to accentuate even further the simplicity of Parisian elegance. Exaggeration of any kind would therefore have been premature, and ridiculous.

However, since one must at all costs create beauty,
and the quest for inventiveness, audacity, and vitality should never
be held back or limited in any way, I created elegant dresses that
were in harmony with the interior decoration of those Frenchwomen
who were still able to entertain guests. Despite all the sad aspects
of the Occupation, we never stopped enriching our collections
with evening dresses that we knew — alas! — would never sell.
But that turned out to be a much more precious asset than one
might have thought. Also, those dresses gave us courage! [36]

You have a reputation for being extremely discreet.

I am talking a great deal about myself. It is not my custom to do so. [37]
I very much prefer that my work shall speak for me. [38]

❦ NOTES ❧

1 Elene Foster, "Six Noted Paris Dressmakers — Madame Jeanne Lanvin," *The Christian Science Monitor*, October 1, 1930, 8.

2 Foster, "Six Noted Paris Dressmakers," 8.

3 Foster, "Six Noted Paris Dressmakers," 8.

4 Foster, "Six Noted Paris Dressmakers," 8.

5 Jeanne Lanvin, "Le Cinéma influence-t-il la Mode?" Le Figaro Illustré, February 1933, 78.

6 Odette Arnaud, "L'Apprentissage," *Miroir du Monde*, September 15, 1934.

7 "Grand concours de la mode. Lanvin," *Le Matin*, May 17, 1923.

8 "Jeanne Lanvin, Robe-de-Style: One mode immune to Time's Whims," *The Washington Post*, August 9, 1938, X9.

9 Mme. Jeanne Lanvin, "Jeanne Lanvin," *The Washington Post*, February 6, 1927.

10 "Jeanne Lanvin, Robe-de-Style: One Mode Immune to Time's Whims."

11 "Jeanne Lanvin, Robe-de-Style: One Mode Immune to Time's Whims."

12 "Jeanne Lanvin, Robe-de-Style: One Mode Immune to Time's Whims."

13 "Jeanne Lanvin, Robe-de-Style: One Mode Immune to Time's Whims."

14 Jean-Louis Vaudoyer, "Madame. . . Jeanne Lanvin," *Vogue* (France), Winter 1946.

15 Foster, "Six Noted Paris Dressmakers."

16 Foster, "Six Noted Paris Dressmakers."

17 Marcel Zahar, "Faut-il poursuivre ou exploiter la copie?" *Vu*, April 5, 1933, 511.

18 Zahar, "Faut-il poursuivre ou exploiter la copie?", 510, 511.

19 Jeanne Lanvin, "Feminine Charm Paramount," *The North China Herald*, August 30, 1933.

20 "Dare's Weekly Fashion Letter, Lanvin's Prophecy," *The Washington Post*, March 30, 1930, S8.

21 Jeanne Lanvin, "Feminine Charm Paramount."

22 Mme. Jeanne Lanvin, "Jeanne Lanvin."

23 "Dare's Weekly Fashion Letter, Lanvin's Prophecy," 58.

24 Ginette Le Prieur, "Jeanne Lanvin habille . . . les jeunes filles de l'écran et les autres," *Ciné France*, October 19, 1938.

25 Jeanne Lanvin, "Feminine Charm Paramount."

26 Mme. Jeanne Lanvin, "Jeanne Lanvin."

27 Mme. Jeanne Lanvin, "Jeanne Lanvin."

28 Paule Hutzler, "Comment nous faisons une Parisienne cent pour cent," *Miroir du Monde*, April 8, 1933, 52.

29 "Waist line going back to normal," *The China Press*, April 26, 1926, 5.

30 Foster, "Six Noted Paris Dressmakers," 8.

31 Foster, "Six Noted Paris Dressmakers," 8.

32 "Dare's Weekly Fashion Letter, Lanvin's Prophecy," S8.

33 Lanvin, "Le Cinéma influence-t-il la Mode?" 78.

34 Le Prieur, "Jeanne Lanvin habille . . . les jeunes filles de l'écran et les autres."

35 Suzanne Fournier, "Jeanne Lanvin vous parle d'élégance," *Modes et travaux*, July 15, 1941, 11.

36 Claude Cézan, *La mode, phénomène humain* (Paris: Privat, 1967), 108.

37 Foster, "Six Noted Paris Dressmakers," 8.

38 Foster, "Six Noted Paris Dressmakers," 8.

MADELEINE VIONNET

Madame Vionnet, you come from eastern France, correct?

I'm a Jura girl, my father came from there. Franche-Comté bred, knucklehead. I was born independent. I have never been able to belong to anyone, not even a husband. I was married twice and I couldn't stand it. Vionnet is my maiden name! I always wanted to keep my own name![1]

Your parents separated when you were three and a half.

My mother left my father because she wanted to work. She wanted to do her own thing. She was a very organized woman; she thrived on responsibility. She founded the Petit Casino, which became one of the best cafés concerts in Paris.[2] She took me to her mother's house in Joigny. Then when I was five, my father came for me.[3]

What did your father do for a living?

He was a toll collector.[4] He lived in Aubervilliers. We had an apartment, with a room for each of us. He was a handsome man.[5]

Tell us how you started out.

By chance. My teacher thought I was talented and wanted me to continue my studies in order to become a schoolteacher, too. But my father didn't think that was a good idea. He listened to the advice of a friend whose wife was a dressmaker. So I was apprenticed to her . . .[6]

Would you have liked to continue school?

Oh yes, and I wept . . . like a schoolgirl . . .[7]

Where did you learn your trade?

My school was the workshop. I started off apprenticing to be a seamstress. Today I regret never having learned to draw — if only because it would allow me to explain myself more quickly.[8]

And where did you acquire your good taste?

Taste is a feeling that allows you to tell the difference between what is beautiful and what is merely spectacular — and also what is ugly! It is passed on from mother to daughter. But some people don't need to be taught: they have innate taste. Like me.[9]

Were you talented?

What a strange thing, talent. I didn't have any. In any case, I didn't know if I had any. I simply knew that I was competent.[10]

At eighteen you married a policeman, Émile Députot,
from whom you were quickly separated. Then you went
to England to learn English and become a première.

I worked five years in London, from the age of twenty to twenty-five.[11]

You answered a classified ad in The Morning Post
and began working for London designer Kate Reily.

I dressed the Rothschild daughter, who married the Duke of
Marlborough. A tall woman. A beautiful, magnificent woman.
I even dressed her for her presentation at court.[12]

*Upon returning to Paris, you worked for two
of the most prestigious couture houses. In 1901,
you were hired by the Callot Soeurs.*

I was *première* in Madame Gerber's own atelier (she was one of the four
Callot sisters). I was in charge of twenty workers. I made bodices and
skirts. I was the first to alter a woman's suit. For it was chez Callot that
I began designing my own models.[13] Madame Gerber was a grande
dame whose profession was her whole life: she adorned the woman,
draped her body with fabric, and did not merely create a suit; she was
a true designer, not a decorator or a painter, like what we have today.[14]
I was schooled in the magnificent. As for my own work, I kept it
simple, but this experience prevented me forever from doing weak
work.[15] I discovered that couture was an art. Without those ladies,
and what they taught me, I would have continued making Fords.
They taught me to produce Rolls-Royces.[16]

Why did you leave and begin working for Jacques Doucet in 1906?

I left the remarkable Madame Gerber, I abandoned her extraordinary
brain because Monsieur Doucet offered me something I had desired for
many years . . . to create my own designs — my designs! All by myself,
with no one telling me what to do![17] He said to me, "Do what you like,
it'll be a young Maison Doucet within the old Maison Doucet."[18] I am
the one who did away with corsets. . . Chez Doucet I presented models
barelegged in sandals.[19] At the time they called me Miss Chestnut, since
my hair, my eyes, and all of my clothes were brown. I was always the first
to come to work and the last to leave and I always went around turning
off all the lights, for I have forever been obsessed with order.[20] One day
. . . I introduced the pencil skirt. I designed it for legendary actress
Lanthelme (whose real name was Mathilde Fossey). I didn't think it
would ever fall out of fashion. It had three overlapping white and striped
chemises de foulard. The vendeuses were terrified. They asked Doucet
to remove it from the collection.[21] The vendeuses would say, speaking
of my designs, "Nobody is going to notice those dresses." It was upset-
ting. Lanthelme said to me, "This is ridiculous, why do you work here?
. . . Why don't you leave Doucet and open your own house?"[22]

Lanthelme introduced you to her husband, Alfred Charles Edwards, founder of the daily newspaper Le Matin, *in the hope of convincing him to back you financially. You needed eight hundred thousand gold francs.*

Edwards said, "Come up with four hundred thousand francs and I'll get you the rest.[23]

Unfortunately they went on a cruise and Lanthelme drowned. Nonetheless, in 1912 you opened your own couture house at 222 rue de Rivoli.

I was bereft. I had nothing, not a sou.[24] Seeing as I intended to leave Doucet, I said to myself, "I need some money." I scraped together three hundred thousand francs, one hundred thousand of which came out of my savings . . . And I opened up a tiny business on rue de Rivoli . . . Life was a bit tough at the time. But I didn't care. I was good-natured. It was nothing to me. One thing and one thing only has ever mattered in my life: my independence.[25] I said to myself, "If I lose three hundred thousand francs . . . no matter, I know how to work; even if my designs are unpopular, I can dress women elsewhere, with other models." . . . I had learned English in London, so I said to myself, "I'll go work in America if the need arises."[26]

How did World War I affect you?

We suffered so much . . . I still get upset just thinking about it.[27] I closed during the war, but my employees wanted to work. I didn't sell dresses: the clients paid my employees directly. I did that not out of charity, but as a service. What I didn't know was that I was also rendering a service to myself, for once the war was over I retained my employees and my clients.[28] I started again on April 18, 1918.[29] My success was like an explosion.[30]

Was it difficult to find a balance between the creative and the business aspects?

In order to survive, a *maison de couture* must find a balance between design and management. You can't have one without the other. If the business is well managed, the designer can let her imagination speak freely and create the next season's models without hindrance.[31]

You produce in excess of six hundred designs yearly.
How do you keep a fresh perspective with that kind of volume?

My first dresses were easy to make . . . They came out of me like bread
from a baker. It was later, at the end of my career, that things became
difficult. Because I had invented everything! I couldn't come up with
anything new.[32] You have to be original, and in order to do that,
I invented a formula: working the material in three directions —
the length, the width, and the bias. The warp and weft, if you will,
and the forty-five-degree angle that bisects them.[33]

What can you tell us about this famed bias cut?

Everything; we did everything. . . But what I did wasn't just fashion;
it was meant to last a whole lifetime.[34] I must say that as far as the
cut is concerned, I believe I discovered everything that is done today.
When I see something, I say to myself, "I did that!" . . . I was obsessed
with my work.[35] Whenever I saw a woman in the street who looked
good, I would follow her, and mentally modify her clothes; I would
dress her to my taste![36]

What else did you invent?

At the time, we lined dresses with crepe de chine; I was the first
to use a bias cut, but only when I had my own atelier and was able
to do as I pleased . . . The bias was supple, easy, and promising.[37]
I would take my muslin, and place it perfectly on the bias, then
I would make notches along the bias line so as not to lose it,
and the bias of the cloth led the way. It guided me.[38]

Could you describe your creative process?

Every day I would sit in my workshop, facing the little wooden mannequin that I used my whole life, and I would drape it; I would rip apart
and remake it . . . until I was satisfied.[39] The designer who creates, who
dresses people for everyday life, proceeds thus: she must have her
premières, her colleagues, and a large quantity of cotton muslin (cloth
that one cuts over and over again); there are several kinds of finishes
depending on whether one wants to make a dress or a fur coat.

The designer will describe to her *premières* in technical terms the dresses suggested to her by her imagination, or better yet, either in miniature or life size, she cuts and pins the muslin herself. The *première* will finish it, then the design will be worked on again and again, and dissected, and discussed until its color and fabric are decided upon. The *première* then orders her seamstresses to put it together, but how many times that dress will be tried, ripped apart, remade; how many times it will go to court to be judged before it is finally accepted! [40]

You're speaking about a certain type of design.

Naturally I'm talking about creating real designs, for there are designs and then there are designs. There are those that one slavishly copies . . . and those that one does from memory . . . and combinations thereof . . . Out of fifty models, ten are "hits" that make me scream in triumph — the dream has come true, the idea has taken shape; twenty stand up to criticism and go on to live their lives, as it were; ten remain hidden away all season . . . and ten (still more) never become what one had hoped they would be . . . and are dead on arrival. [41] I made dresses mostly. I had one workshop for suits and I don't know how many others for dresses — around twenty. [42] We always had at least five different colors for each model. [43] Honestly, is it easy to create? In my own case, I think not, and I believe that all research is arduous and almost always frustrating. A true creation must necessarily and naturally be laborious. She who attempts to create must suffer. [44]

You've had several partnerships with other designers,
which raises the question of intellectual property.

This is a very legitimate question . . . Is the seamstress or the designer the creator of a model? . . . The designer may well have a rich imagination in terms of color or cloth, but be clueless as to the natural "direction" of a fabric. . . Therefore, ideally the designer should also be a seamstress, though even then she might be surprised to see what her sketches become. On the other hand, the seamstress who creates her own model might encounter unexpected difficulties when she attempts to put it all together — though she should be able to solve those problems quickly. [45]

*Could you tell us something about your
relationship to your premières?*

The *premières* are crucial. They are the ones who prepare the muslin,
but their imagination and taste are always subordinate to the designer
and the house for which they work. I think that some of them
probably suffer due to this. I know for a fact that in my house, among
my *premières* or my seamstresses, the one who creates a style other
than mine will, following the inexorable logistics of our profession,
soon be looking for a new job.[46] For the one who will take my place
tomorrow and force me into retirement — she exists, she is some-
where, the one who will be successful in ten or fifteen years, she may
well be working for me without my knowing it. I am extremely afraid
of that, and that is why I follow everything with an eagle eye . . . and
yet I am always amenable to giving someone a chance: sometimes
I allow a dress to be made, thinking, "She may well be the one."[47]

*As early as the 1920s you set up an emergency fund for your
employees, gave them maternity leave, and provided them
with medical and dental care — a truly pioneering approach.*

This is all quite natural . . . and hardly worth mentioning. One must
do all one can to ensure that one's workers are in good health, for one
must be in good health to successfully pursue a profession as tiring,
exhilarating, and interesting as couture.[48]

Did you work hard at design?

I worked every day of my life. I had saleswomen, a huge staff, but
I worked constantly. My studio had three doors, and they were always
closed. . . Nobody had the right to come in. I was free, tranquil.
At collection time, I was always ready because I kept working all along.[49]

What motivates you?

The ultimate goal in our profession is to create dresses that make the
body and figure look nice, to create beauty. And that's it![50] I am more
a sculptor than a painter. . . I am more sensitive to form than to color.[51]

Fabric is of utmost importance, is it not?

No, I just need to make sure that my materials are of excellent quality. Much as I did for women, I strove to free fabric from the limitations that were forced upon it . . . I proved that fabric falling freely on a body liberated from a heavy armature was beautiful in and of itself. I attempted to bring to fabric a balance that movement in no way altered, but rather magnified.[52] I prefer plain fabrics whose patterns never inhibit the lines, rather than fabrics that can be used in all directions — but most of all I like fabrics that flow.[53] In my youth, all dresses went straight with the grain. We used the material the way it was; what I did with cloth was to make it do what I wanted. I liked flexible cloth that obeyed my hands' commands, that was tightly woven and did not give in easily. . . But I have yet to encounter a cloth that disobeys my orders.[54]

*Your dresses are purist, yet you use
decorative elements from time to time.*

I never looked for it, but I used it on one condition: that it uphold
the architecture of the dress and improve and exalt the whole.[55]

Do you have a favorite color?

More than anything, I like the purity of plain colors. Black,
white — beautiful, sincere tones. Blues and greens that go with the
eyes, reds that echo the lips; what I don't like are ambiguous colors.[56]

Do you think of your customers while creating your models?

For me, the customer is of vital importance. She ceaselessly goads me
toward perfection. It is for her that I attempt to revitalize my work,
while remaining true to myself.[57] Though I don't believe that fashion
magazines are useful in any way, I do believe that there should be as
many fashions as there are types of women. I think of all these women
when I create a collection, and I demand of my profession that it
allow me to show off all different kinds of women. All my life I have
attempted to be the doctor of line, and in my role of doctor, I have
wanted to force my clients to respect their bodies, to exercise, to take
rigorous care of themselves, and to be rid once and for all of the
artificial armatures that deform them.[58]

What advice do you have for potential customers?

They should be content with one or two perfect garments,
rather than falling for perpetual change.[59]

Do you have a feminine ideal?

I never had a neck, and I love necks. I was short, and I need tall
women. Also, I never made dresses for myself.[60] As for forms in
general, I don't have any preconceived notions. I believe that ample
shapes can both conceal and accommodate; but on perfect bodies,
close-fitting, harmonious folds are indescribably beautiful.[61] They
always said I loved women too much! Most of all, Argentine women
. . . with their undulating carnivore backsides.[62]

Do you have any thoughts on contemporary couture?

True couture? Is it mine? Is it today's? Hard to say . . . Couture . . . is a business! . . . When talking about an artist, you're talking about someone, a person, but when speaking about a couturier, you're speaking about a house: it's a business.[63] In the old days, couture was about women; we women were close to our customers and to the cloth.[64]

Why did you decide to close your house?

I had 1,200 employees; none of my peers had as many as I, at that time, in the late 1920s, early 1930s. I closed in 1939 because my company charter was expiring, and my lease was up on avenue Montaigne. . . And also because I had had enough.[65] I never regretted anything, I never reproached myself as regards my employees — nor for anything else. I am not jealous; I am not envious; nothing about my life is difficult to bear. When the time comes, I will gladly pay my dues.[66]

Do you have any advice for young people who would like to work in fashion?

I've always been hard on myself. I believe you have to excel and to excel you have to start by realizing yourself.[67]

You are very involved in the fight against counterfeiting in the fashion industry.

I loathe injustice.[68] Someone who copies models to make money without expending any energy or putting any work into it is a thief.[69] For copying — the worm in the apple — is destroying not only the livelihood of two million employees who work in the various luxury industries, but the very best of our talent. The destruction wrought by piracy is having tremendous impact on French production.[70] My battle cry is "Death to the copyists!" I know I'm going a bit far here, but I can't help it; it expresses my goal, which is to put illicit copyists out of business . . . We are suffering from a sickness that must be eradicated. We need the antidote. We are being robbed.[71]

I would like to ask the public to understand that the applied arts (couture, fashion, decoration) and the fine arts (painting, sculpture) are kith and kin and need to be treated in the same way. I would like to explain that counterfeiting puts people out of work; I'd like to point out that there is a difference between borrowing and outright stealing:[72] there are those who present models and say who they are stolen from; there are those who present models without saying anything; there is the indelicate employee who takes models to the copier and who is his accomplice; there is the seamstress who can reproduce certain models by heart. How to classify all these cases? Again, I leave that up to our lawmakers.[73]

How would you define fashion?

For me "fashion" means nothing more than general, universal ideas that are part and parcel of the immutable and eternal character of pure beauty.[74] Fashion does not exist; personally, I hate fashion! One finds all kinds of styles in my work... One need only choose: everything depends on your particular aesthetic.[75]

And how about today's fashion?

But it is not fashion. It's honest work, nothing more. It has nothing to do with the refinement that used to go into dressing.[76]

If you could start again, how would you go about it?

I would continue to follow my system: supple dresses that exalt the body. But the thing that might prevent me from working would be the lack of personnel.[77]

Whose clothes do you wear?

Balenciaga... He is a good friend... Comes to see me regularly and sends me what he thinks I need and can wear.[78] He was the last of our great designers. Fashion and the reign of the elegant woman came to an end with him.[79]

How do you feel now that you've reached the age of ninety-nine?

I was born energetic, and I remain energetic. I still have my wits about me. I have not slowed down in the slightest. I am completely lucid; I would even say that age has made me more lucid than ever.[80]

Any last words?

The art of dressing takes time and patience.[81]

—⟨ NOTES ⟩—

1 Marie Lavie-Compin, "Madeleine Vionnet, Pour l'année du flou, l'année Vionnet," *Vogue* France, April 1974, 116.

2 Célia Bertin, *Haute Couture, Terre inconnue* (Paris: Hachette, 1956), 162.

3 Madeleine Vionnet, interview by Madeleine Chapsal, January 30, 1974, transcript, Madeleine Chapsal archives, 2.

4 Madeleine Vionnet, interview by Madeleine Chapsal, January 30, 1974, 4.

5 Madeleine Vionnet, interview by Madeleine Chapsal, January 30, 1974, 2.

6 Gaston Derys, "En devisant avec... Madeleine Vionnet," *Minerva, Supplément féminin illustré du Journal de Rouen*, January 2, 1938, 7.

7 Derys, "En devisant avec... Madeleine Vionnet," 7.

8 Derys, "En devisant avec... Madeleine Vionnet," 7.

9 Madeleine Chapsal, "Hommage à Madeleine Vionnet," *Vogue* France, April 1975, 26.

10 Madeleine Vionnet, interview by Madeleine Chapsal, circa 1960, transcript, Madeleine Chapsal archives.

11 Madeleine Vionnet, interview by Madeleine Chapsal, circa 1960.

12 Madeleine Vionnet, interview by Madeleine Chapsal, circa 1960.

13 M.-A. Dabadie, "Madeleine Vionnet, 'la grande dame de la couture' fête ses 90 ans," *Le Figaro*, June 11–12, 1966.

14 Bertin, 162.

15 Biche, "La vie et le secret de Madeleine Vionnet," *Marie Claire*, May 28, 1937, 11.

16 Anne Manson, "Elle fête aujourd'hui ses 90 ans, Madeleine Vionnet qui fut la grande dame de la couture entre les deux guerres : J'ai vécu l'âge d'or de l'élégance," *L'Aurore*, June 22, 1966.

17 André Beucler, Chez Madeleine Vionnet, circa 1929–30, transcript, André Beucler archives, 24.

18 Madeleine Vionnet, interview by Madeleine Chapsal, circa 1960.

19 Bertin, 161.

20 Manson, "Elle fête aujourd'hui ses 90 ans, Madeleine Vionnet qui fut la grande dame de la couture entre les deux guerres : J'ai vécu l'âge d'or de l'élégance."

21 Dabadie, "Madeleine Vionnet, 'la grande dame de la couture' fête ses 90 ans."

22 Madeleine Vionnet, interview by Madeleine Chapsal, circa 1960, 21, 23.

23 Madeleine Vionnet, interview by Madeleine Chapsal, circa 1960, 21.

24 Madeleine Vionnet, interview by Madeleine Chapsal, circa 1960, 22.

25 Madeleine Vionnet, interview by Madeleine Chapsal, circa 1960, 22.

26 Madeleine Vionnet, interview by Madeleine Chapsal, circa 1960, 25.

27 Madeleine Vionnet, interview by Madeleine Chapsal, circa 1960, 15.

28 Madeleine Vionnet, interview by Madeleine Chapsal, circa 1960, 15–16.

29 Lucie Noel, "Grande Dame of Designers," *Irish Independent*, July 22, 1966.

30 Bernard Nevill, "Vionnet," *Vogue* (UK), October 1, 1967, 134.

31 Madeleine Vionnet, "Cri de ralliement! La couture et les copieurs," *Le Moniteur de l'exportation et la revue artistique réunis*, May 1920, 4.

32 Madeleine Vionnet, interview by Madeleine Chapsal, circa 1960.

33 Beucler, Chez Madeleine Vionnet, 19.

34 Madeleine Vionnet, interview by Madeleine Chapsal, circa 1960, 26.

35 Madeleine Vionnet, interview by Madeleine Chapsal, circa 1960.

36 Chapsal, "Hommage à Madeleine Vionnet," 26.

37 Lavie-Compin, "Madeleine Vionnet, Pour l'année du flou, l'année Vionnet," 117.

38 Lavie-Compin, "Madeleine Vionnet, Pour l'année du flou, l'année Vionnet," 117.

39 D. Paulvé, "Madeleine Vionnet," *Marie-France*, March 1974, 73.

40 Madeleine Vionnet, interview by Madeleine Chapsal, January 30, 1974, 4.

41 Madeleine Vionnet, interview by Madeleine Chapsal, January 30, 1974, 4.

42 Lavie-Compin, "Madeleine Vionnet, Pour l'année du flou, l'année Vionnet," 117.

43 Paulvé, "Madeleine Vionnet," 73.

44 Vionnet, "Cri de ralliement! La couture et les copieurs," 5.

45 Vionnet, "Cri de ralliement! La couture et les copieurs," 4.

46 Vionnet, "Cri de ralliement! La couture et les copieurs," 4.

47 Beucler, Chez Madeleine Vionnet, 23.

48 Derys, "En devisant avec. . .
    Madeleine Vionnet."

49 Hebe Dorsey, "The Inventor of the
    Bias Cut," *The International Herald
    Tribune*, February 6, 1973.

50 Derys, "En devisant avec. . .
    Madeleine Vionnet," 70.

51 Alain Bernard, "Quarante ans de métier,
    Madeleine Vionnet, créatrice de la femme
    en biais débuta apprentie pour finir
    Reine de la couture," *Radio*, 1948.

52 Biche, "La vie et le secret de
    Madeleine Vionnet," 11, 46.

53 Derys, "En devisant avec. . .
    Madeleine Vionnet," 70.

54 Lavie-Compin, "Madeleine Vionnet,
    Pour l'année du flou, l'année Vionnet," 117.

55 Biche, "La vie et le secret
    de Madeleine Vionnet," 11, 46.

56 Biche, "La vie et le secret
    de Madeleine Vionnet," 11, 46.

57 Biche, "La vie et le secret
    de Madeleine Vionnet," 11.

58 Biche, "La vie et le secret
    de Madeleine Vionnet," 11.

59 Biche, "La vie et le secret
    de Madeleine Vionnet," 11.

60 Madeleine Vionnet, interview
    by Madeleine Chapsal, circa 1960, 25.

61 Biche, "La vie et le secret de
    Madeleine Vionnet," 11, 46.

62 Bruce Chatwin, *What Am I Doing Here*
    (London: Penguin Books, 1989), 90–91.

63 Madeleine Vionnet, interview
    by Madeleine Chapsal, circa 1960.

64 Madeleine Vionnet, interview
    by Madeleine Chapsal, circa 1960.

65 Lavie-Compin, "Madeleine Vionnet,
    Pour l'année du flou, l'année Vionnet," 117.

66 Lavie-Compin, "Madeleine Vionnet,
    Pour l'année du flou, l'année Vionnet," 117.

67 Chapsal, "Hommage á
    Madeleine Vionnet," 25.

68 Madeleine Vionnet, interview by
    Madeleine Chapsal, January 30, 1974.

69 Vionnet, "Cri de ralliement!
    La couture et les copieurs," 6.

70 Madeleine Vionnet, "Copie," (brochure), 7.

71 Vionnet, "Cri de ralliement!
    La couture et les copieurs," 5.

72 Vionnet, "Cri de ralliement!
    La couture et les copieurs," 5.

73 Vionnet, "Cri de ralliement!
    La couture et les copieurs," 6.

74 Biche, "La vie et le secret de
    Madeleine Vionnet," 11.

75 Beucler, Chez Madeleine Vionnet, 18.

76 Paulvé, "Madeleine Vionnet," 73.

77 Madeleine Vionnet, interview
    by Madeleine Chapsal, circa 1960, 26.

78 Noel, "Grande Dame of Designers."

79 Paulvé, "Madeleine Vionnet," 73.

80 Lavie-Compin, "Madeleine Vionnet,
    Pour l'année du flou, l'année Vionnet," 116.

81 Biche, "La vie et le secret de
    Madeleine Vionnet," 46.

GABRIELLE
CHANEL

Mademoiselle Chanel . . .

I cannot sit down and tell anyone, especially a stranger, the story of my life. There is my work. Judge that.[1]

Nevertheless, could you describe the beginning of your long career?

I would begin thus: "Today, I decided to . . ." I don't think I could start to talk about it using any word other than *today*. I don't know how to inhabit any other time or place than the present. When I am elsewhere, I get bored. And I hate being bored . . . Today, I feel like working. I am beginning work on my spring collection. The first model I make is always for me.[2]

Why did you decide to become a designer?

I wanted to be independent. I absolutely wanted to work.[3]

It's almost as if you didn't have a choice.

When work is to be had, you've got to take it. If you mistreat your work, it will mistreat you.[4]

When you started out, the profession was no doubt quite different from what it is today.

When I started out, one did not receive fashion designers. I'm the one who changed all that. Jacques Doucet was a man no one said hello to, yet he turned out to be a great art collector.[5] Today things go so fast. Life goes too fast. No one takes the time.[6]

Are you proud of the fashion house that you built?

It's the only thing that is truly mine. People wanted to give me things, but I didn't want anything from anyone. I built the House of Chanel all by myself. I didn't have a financial backer. None of that. Nobody had to pay anything — just a line of credit from a bank that I never overdrew.[7]

You gave yourself wholeheartedly to the endeavor.

I could never give up the House of Chanel. It was my child. I created it. From nothing, from rags.[8]

What was your goal when you founded your fashion house?

I always wanted to design dresses that women could wear for years. Is it pretentious of me to say that I succeeded in doing so? Dress a woman today and she'll be dressed tomorrow, too. It's the paradox of style. Much like the ephemeral, nothing lasts longer than the present. The true artist is not ahead of his time. He belongs to his time.[9]

*However, one needs to know the past
to move forward, don't you think?*

The same designers who incessantly talk about "designing for the future"
should look at the history of design. Those who don't design for today
don't design for tomorrow. In reality, they belong to yesterday.[10]
All children know that tomorrow never comes. Yesterday and tomorrow
have this in common: they are not today. A dress or a suit should always
belong to today, like a scent lingering in the air.[11]

By all accounts you had a difficult childhood.

They say that I am from the Auvergne. And yet nothing about me
brings to mind the Auvergne. My mother came from there. I hated it.
I was drowning in sadness, and horror. I can't tell you how many times
I decided to kill myself. *That poor Jeanne* — I couldn't stand hearing
my mother referred to in that manner. Like all children, I eaves-
dropped on my parents. I learned that my father had bankrupted
my mother, *poor Jeanne*. Yet she married the man she loved. And to
hear that I was an orphan! People felt sorry for me. I didn't think
I deserved their pity, since I had a father. All of this was deeply
humiliating. I didn't understand that I wasn't loved, and that
I was being looked after out of charity.[12]
    I wanted love. I didn't get it. I used to set traps for it.
Later, I suppose, there was more love that I wanted. I had a horrible
childhood. My aunts wanted me to stay in from five in the afternoon
and prepare my trousseau. Finally I escaped them and came to Paris,
my bag packed with only one dress, but a great many lies.[13]

Indeed, you are a notoriously unreliable narrator.

I never told the truth even to my priest.[14] I talk a lot of rubbish.[15]

Is Coco a nickname you acquired in childhood, or later in life?

My father was dead-set against my being called Gaby, which is short for Gabrielle. He called me *petit Coco*, thinking that another nickname would come along. He hated Gabrielle, which he hadn't chosen, and he was right. After a while petit disappeared, and I was just plain Coco. It was grotesque. I would love to be rid of it, but I don't suspect I ever will.[16]

Your middle name is Bonheur, which is French for "happiness."

Happiness is an illusion. Blessed are those who are not aware of this.[17] I am not, I warn you, a happy woman.[18] Few people suspect it, but I have never known happiness.[19] At the age of six, I am already alone. My mother has just died. My father deposits me, like a millstone, at the house of my aunts, and leaves immediately for an America from which he will never return. An orphan . . . ever since then, this word has always paralyzed me with fear; even now I cannot go past a girls' boarding school and hear people saying, "they are orphans," without tears coming to my eyes.[20]

As you yourself have often said, you were never a happy woman; yet in view of your considerable success, you seem to have been no stranger to luck.

I have always been remarkably lucky! I never won a bet, but thankfully I am not the gambling type! I love my job, and I am lucky enough to have been successful . . . This proves that one should concentrate one's ambitions on things that one loves. For I am convinced that the fact of loving what you do generates its own kind of luck; otherwise one's enthusiasm wanes.[21]

Why did you decide to remain single? You surely could have married many times over.

The two men I loved never understood it. They were rich men, and they didn't understand why a woman who would have money would want to work.[22]

One of those men was the Duke of Westminster.

I was lucky to have known the duke. Fourteen years. That is a long time, no? He was shy and timid, too, but I have never felt so protected. He was solid and comfortable. He understood me — except for my working, of course. He gave me peace. He was generous. He was simple. We talked half in English, half in French. "I don't want you to learn English," he said, "and discover there is nothing in the conversation you hear around us. . .

Toward the end, it almost seemed as if we were looking for little things to quarrel about, even though it was always in an undertone. The duke continued to talk of marriage, and if I had had children, I would have married. But my child was the House of Chanel.[23]

If I am not mistaken, the other man in your life was also English.

The name of the handsome Englishman was Boy Capel. He didn't know what to do with me either. He took me to Paris and set me up in a hotel. . . These men thought of me as a poor, abandoned sparrow; in actual fact, I was a monster. I gradually learned about life, I mean how to cope with it. I was highly intelligent, far more intelligent than I am now. I was unlike anyone else, either physically or mentally. I liked solitude; instinctively I loved what was beautiful and loathed prettiness.[24]

He enabled you to set up your first business.

One day, I said to Boy Capel: "I'm going to work. I want to make hats." His response: "Fine. You'll do very well. You'll get through a lot of money, but that doesn't matter, you need to keep busy, it's an excellent idea. The most important thing is that you're happy."

The women I saw at the races wore enormous loaves on their heads, constructions made of feathers and improved with fruits and plumes; but worst of all, which appalled me, their hats did not fit on their heads.[25]

It seems as if it all happened very fast.

I rented the first floor of a building in the rue Cambon. I still have it.
On the door, it read: CHANEL, MODES. Capel put an excellent woman
at my disposal, Madame Aubert, whose real name was Mademoiselle
de Saint-Pons. She advised me and guided me. In the grandstands, people
began talking about my amazing, unusual hats, so neat and austere, which
were somehow a foretaste of the Iron Age that was to come, but which had
not yet dawned. Customers came, initially prompted by curiosity. One day
I had a visit from one such woman, who admitted quite openly: "I came . . .
to have a look at you." I was the curious creature, the little woman whose
straw boater fitted her head, and whose head fitted her shoulders.[26]

Barely two years later you began designing clothes.

1914. The war. Capel persuaded me to withdraw to Deauville, where
he rented a villa for his ponies. Many elegant ladies had come to
Deauville. Not only did they need to have hats made for them, but
soon, because there were no dressmakers, they had to be properly
attired. I only had milliners with me; I converted them into dressmakers. There was a shortage of material. I cut jerseys for them from
the sweaters the stable lads wore and from the knitted training
garments that I wore myself. By the end of the first summer of the
war, I had earned two hundred thousand gold francs.[27]

That was quite a tidy sum at that time.

Money is the key to freedom.[28]

So, there you were, working in fashion.

What did I know about my new profession? Nothing. I didn't
know dressmakers existed. Did I have any idea of the revolution
that I was about to stir up? By no means. One world was ending,
another was about to be born. I was in the right place; an opportunity beckoned, I took it. I had grown up with this new century:
I was, therefore, the one to be consulted about its sartorial style.
What was needed was simplicity, comfort, and neatness: unwittingly,
I offered all of that.[29]

Can you tell us something about your training?

I was self-taught. I learned badly, haphazardly. And yet, when life put me in touch with those who were the most delightful or brilliant people of my age, a Stravinsky, or a Picasso, I neither felt stupid, nor embarrassed. Why? Because I had worked out on my own that which cannot be taught. I will return to this frequently. For the time being, I want to end on this important aphorism, which is the secret of my success, and perhaps that of civilization; confronted with ruthless techniques of doing things: it's with what cannot be taught that one succeeds.[30]

You must have had a hard time at first.

I had no idea what was going on, but once I understood the game, everything went well.[31]

You have been strongly critical of some of your colleagues.

After 1920 the great couturiers tried to fight back. At about that time, I remember contemplating the auditorium at the Opéra from the back of a box. All those gaudy, resuscitated colors shocked me; those reds, those greens, those electric blues, the entire Rimsky-Korsakov and Gustave Moreau palette, brought back into fashion by Paul Poiret, made me feel ill. The Ballets Russes were stage decor, not couture. I remember only too well saying to someone sitting beside me: These colors are impossible. I'm bloody well going to dress them in black.[32]

Tell me about your creative process.

You know, I can't sew, not even a button.[33] I sketch very little. . . Dress designing is not sketching. It is not art. It is taste, plus a sense of professionalism.[34] I work directly on the body. I draw inspiration from my models, not from documents. That is why I change models so often. I work with a pair of scissors and lots of pins. . . I work and work on the model. Then I see something in her cheek or that a certain collar looks good on her, and I work and work until I have a dress for her. When someone tells me a dress is good, I want to rip it apart. It always looks good when it is pinned together, but you must put a woman in it. It must be sewn, lined, then proportioned to the body. That's what finally makes it look good or bad.[35]

Do you have a sort of secret recipe?

I will tell you a secret. I always try the first models on myself in the studio. That way, I get the right proportions and feel the fit, the ease, the weight of the dress myself.[36]

Trick question: How long will dresses be this season?

I order my employees to never answer idiotic questions concerning the length of the skirts. How important can that be? The thing I'm concerned with is that my dresses not fall out of fashion twenty years after they were designed.[37]

However, there is a part of the body that you always hide, and that you apparently despise: the knees.

But do you know of many women of fifty, or even forty, who have good knees, or any women at all who are no longer young girls? Very few. They are either too fat or too scrawny — it is odd, no? Why show them?[38] You know what happens when I enter a restaurant? Men look at me and applaud because I said it is horrible to show one's knee. It is as though one showed one's elbows.[39]

Your thoughts on the miniskirt?

An exhibition of meat.[40] A woman cannot sit comfortably in a miniskirt. If being modern means adapting to one's era, how can being modern mean wearing a dress that you can't even sit down in (and I'm not talking about decency)? You have to be able to both walk and sit in a dress.[41]

So, the key to being modern lies in the ability to move about freely?

A woman should be able to move any way she wants without her clothing moving. The other day I saw one of my girlfriends sitting stock-still. "What's the matter?" I asked her. "Are you sick?" "No," she said, "I'm wearing a new dress."[42] Do you remember the "New Look" — the fashion of the hidden corset and the skirt that swept the floor? Women ended up just saying no to this. So today we have the "New New Look" — the dress itself has turned into a mid-thigh corset. Style is so much more than that. It's the cut. It's the proportions, the colors, the fabric. And more than anything else, the entire woman in and of herself.[43]

You have often addressed the subject of copying.

Few designers have been copied as much as I have, and it has always given me great joy. I always side with the majority. I believe that style belongs to the street, in everyday life, like a revolution. That's the real style. When style comes from the street, it's a bad omen. Fashion becomes outdated, but the style remains, for a long time.[44] That being said, I don't design for a couple of old hags.[45] I get copied — plundered sometimes — but no one imitates me.[46]

Is that copying akin to theft?

I prefer copying to stealing. Now there is a difference for you! Seriously, there are forty thousand little seamstresses in France. Where can they find their ideas, if not among us? Let them copy. I a on the side of women and seamstresses, not fashion houses.[47]

So, being copied doesn't bother you?

Every imitation has its basis in love for the original.[48]

Do you have any recurring sources of inspiration?

Indirectly, it was my Auvergne aunts who imposed their modesty on the beautiful Parisian ladies. Years have gone by, and it is only now that I realize that the austerity of dark shades, the respect for colors borrowed from nature, the almost monastic cut of my summer alpaca wear and of my winter tweed suits, all that puritanism that elegant ladies would go crazy for, came from Mont-Dore. If I wore hats pulled down over my head, it is because the wind in the Auvergne might mess up my hair. I was a Quaker woman who was conquering Paris, just as the stiff Genevese or American cowl had conquered Versailles 150 years previously.[49]

How important is Paris in contemporary fashion?

These days, while countries the world over are gung-ho on exporting their traditions, agriculture and own particular genius, it's more important than ever for us to defend the spirit of Paris, rather than a few innovations. Let us remain the instigators of the ephemeral rather than vainly attempting to stabilize that which is inherently unstable, and to codify fashion. The genius of the French, in matters of fashion, has always been to be its wellspring. Draw as much water as you want, but you can't walk off with the fountain.[50]

One doesn't create fashions for Paris or for the rest of the world; one doesn't guide the aspirations of one's era, one doesn't make eternal art. One can only interpret the aesthetic desire of a certain time period. Fashion springs up each season like a flower in the garden of the universe. And yet, just about anywhere in the world, women will admire a simple ribbon by saying, "It comes from Paris."[51]

Do you feel that other couturiers have followed you on this point?

I would have liked to work alongside my rivals, in order to coordinate our efforts into a perfect whole: French fashion. I would like to help certain generous men understand that it is just as important to buy a simple, well-made dress for their lady as it is to buy her a fur coat, a car, or a jewel. A dress is chic not because it is pretentious, but because it is made with quality material, and because of the cut and the form. Better to have two perfect dresses than four mediocre ones.[52]

Does fashion have a nationality?

Originality has no nationality or place or origin. When I began in Paris, there were a Spaniard and five Italians among the French fashion designers.[53]

Which colleagues of yours do you admire?

There is no more competition. You have no idea how hard it is to work without competition . . . I continue to work though, to stave off boredom.[54]

There must be a designer you admire.

Balenciaga is the only designer I admire.[55]

And what about the new generation?

Saint Laurent has excellent taste. The more he copies me the better taste he displays.[56]

Are couturiers artists in their own right?

We are not artists. We are artisans, workers with taste.[57] The thing about authentic works of art is that they are ugly before becoming beautiful, whereas fashion looks beautiful before becoming ugly. No need to be a genius to create fashions; you just need professional experience, and a little taste.[58]

How would you define yourself?

Look at me: this is what you call a lady who designs clothes. A simple worker. I am a worker. Some people don't like that word, but I do.[59]

Should fashion be considered an art?

Look at the current talk about Art. Art with a capital A. It has become the excuse for everything. . . We would be wise to take a vacation from it. Why be saturated by it? The result is that everything becomes not art, but artistic.[60] Unlike the other arts, fashion is beholden to time — to the very minute in which it is born; it has the frail elegance of those gods who die young. After all, our business consists of destroying that which we have just created.[61]

Do you see fashion as more of a craft than an art?

I repeat: couture is a technique, a business, a job. It may be
that there is an awareness of art, which is already a great deal,
that it excites artists, that it accompanies them in their cars, on the
path to glory; that a bonnet with ribbons should be immortalized
in an Ingres drawing, or a hat in a Renoir, so much the better, but it's
an accident; it's as if a dragonfly had mistaken Monet's *Water Lilies*
for the real thing and had alighted there. If an outfit attempts to
match a fine, statuesque body or to enhance a sublime heroine,
that's wonderful, but it does not justify couturiers persuading
themselves or thinking of themselves — or dressing or posing
— as artists . . . they'll eventually fail as artists.[62]

*Your generation of fashion designers included an
unprecedented number of exceptionally talented women.*

How could a man ever design women's clothes? A man doesn't grasp
the importance of a pretty, long neck, or the significance of emphasizing the length of the leg, and how one shouldn't widen the shoulders, and not exaggerate the outline of the bust, and to make jackets
in which you can raise your arms.[63]

What is fashion?

Fashion? Whenever anyone asks me what I think of fashion, I don't
even understand the question . . . What is fashion? Once in a while I will
change a small detail, the collar, the arm — this is very important in
a dress — and a minute later, everything else is no longer in fashion . . .
But this is done to improve the dress. I never sat around thinking how
I was going to change this or that aspect of fashion![64] Fashion exists
so that it can become outmoded. I always design clothes for tomorrow.[65]

*If you were to emphasize one thing in today's blurred
fashion landscape, what would it be?*

The most important thing to remember about fashion is that
it isn't always right to be always in fashion.[66]

What is your take on contemporary fashion?

Fashion is confused these days. As for me, I'm doing what is simple, elegant, and practical.[67]

What has your lifelong approach to fashion been?

The luxury of ease and comfort.[68]

Then what is your definition of luxury?

I have always believed that good manners, good food, and good humor in social settings are the three essential elements of French luxury. This is an ethical issue, and not always noticeable; and very simple, natural, subtle people have these qualities in abundance their whole lives, and manage to enjoy an elegance that has nothing to do with money . . . thank God.[69]

Should fashion look to the past?

Fashion should never be retrospective. It becomes a disguise that way, and disguises are horrible.[70]

What approach to fashion should a woman take?

I hate seeing women who are obsessed with being fashionable to the point of neglecting their own personalities; I fear that they are a little too influenced by the Americans. These women would do better to help us spread French elegance all over the world. Fashion has always been quintessentially French and we should keep it that way.[71]

I see old ladies wearing dresses that show far too much of their décolleté. Who wants to see that? As for the young ones: they have been told that unless they show a good half of their bosoms outside their dresses no man will look at them or make love to them.[72]

*You have often been criticized for presenting what
seems to be the same style over and over.*

My designs are similar in the sense that a woman's body always
remains a woman's body.[73] Those who say, "Chanel is okay, but it's
always the same thing," don't understand anything about modern life.
Do men's fashions change every season? They need a dinner suit,
a tuxedo, and perhaps a tailcoat. And women today lead lives that
are similar to men's: they need sport suits, business suits, a "tuxedo,"
and an elegant dress that is the female equivalent of "tails." But very
feminine, with jewels and bright colors.[74]

Your goal seems always to be the same.

My only goal is to dress women's bodies in the best way possible:
to accentuate their busts, raise their waists, free their arms, and
lengthen their legs from their hips to the tips of their toes, thus
allowing them to move about freely.[75] The dress shouldn't wear
the woman; it's the woman who should wear the dress.[76]

Are you a passionate woman?

Everything I do, I do with passion. Every single thing I decide to do,
I do while telling myself that my life depends on this one isolated thing.[77]

What is elegance in your conception of fashion?

The truly courageous act is to smile. True modesty, beauty, and
morality consist in keeping one's problems and worries to oneself
and being supremely polite.[78] Your dresses and finery need to be
as integral a part of you as your very gestures, your walk, or your
smile. It is only in that way that they will make you more beautiful,
instead of disguising you.

Brummel's definition still holds today: True elegance consists in not being noticed.[79] No dressmaker, no makeup artist, no amount of money can make you charming. The art is to find it in yourself.[80] It is not money. It is not the contrary of poverty. It is the contrary of vulgarity — and negligence. You can always be overdressed, but never too elegant.[81]

Is the concept of beauty still important these days?

The word beauty has become hollow. Today, everybody talks about shock value. But what is more shocking than beauty? Either art has taught us this, or it has taught us absolutely nothing. A touch of beauty or elegance has the same fantastical power as a candle flame in a dark room. And God knows that darkness has been making more and more inroads of late.[82]

What about physical beauty?

In the course of my life I have known many beautiful women and stunning boys, and let me tell you: beauty is not enough.[83] Beauty can be very boring. Charm is always seductive. And a woman must always be natural.[84] If you are ugly, eventually people will cease noticing it, but never if you are negligent.[85]

How do you feel about aging?

Age doesn't count: you can be ravishing at twenty, charming at forty, and irresistible the rest of your life.[86] The surest way to grow old psychologically is to lie about your age. But then, it is no one else's business, is it?[87] In the end, we're all as old as we deserve to be.[88]

What is the most common mistake women make?

As they grow older, the mistake most women make is to want to appear younger than they are. On the contrary, when one is no longer young one should attempt to appear older.[89]

If you could choose another career, what would it be?

I would have loved a profession in which I would have been all by myself, without depending on anyone else, alone, and free.[90]

What makes you happy?

Couture is my joy, my goal, my ideal, my raison d'être, my life, my everything, my deepest self.[91]

And what about love?

A woman who has a man who loves her and makes her feel beautiful has no need whatsoever for a beauty salon. But without that, she dies. A woman needs to be stroked from her hair to her feet; otherwise she will be frustrated . . . Me, I'm not frustrated. I had lovers . . . But "it" hasn't happened to me for a long time, except in dreams. I wake up, saying, "Oh, come off it, old woman!"[92]

So, you don't feel lonely?

I am alone because in every man a pimp is lurking.[93]

Does money change the dynamic between people?

There are those with money and those who are rich. They are not the same people. Only the rich give.[94]

What still surprises you?

I don't understand how a woman can go out without making an effort to look nice, if only out of politeness. How pretentious one has to be to show oneself like that, without anything! And then, you never know: you might have a rendezvous with fate that day, and you'd better be as nice-looking as possible — for fate's sake.[95]

What advice do you have for our readers?

Cultivate yourself, for yourself: but above all keep your sense of humor. Learn everything: then forget it. Remember less; understand more. Memory in a woman is the end of the girl.[96] Be true to yourself. Then at least one person will not be false with you.[97]

What should one be wary of?

Beware of mirrors; they only reflect the image you have of yourself.[98]

Last words?

I have dressed the whole world, and now it goes about naked.[99]

⟞ NOTES ⟝

1   Joseph Barry, "An Interview with Chanel," McCall's, November 1965, 121.

2   Jean Denys, "La femme la plus écoutée des femmes — Chanel aujourd'hui," *Elle* (France), December 17, 1958, 49.

3   Coco Chanel, "La mode, Qu'est que c'est?" On side 1 of sound recording *Coco Chanel Parle*. Hugues Desalle.

4   Claude Berthod, "Qui était la vraie Chanel? Psychanalyse d'un monstre sacré," *Elle* (France), November 8, 1971, 38.

5   Madeleine Chapsal, "Reportage Chanel au travail," *L'Express*, August 11, 1960, 16.

6   Lucie Noël, "Grand Mademoiselle Coco Chanel She Twice Conquered Fashion World," *The Herald Tribune*, August 4, 1960.

7   Chanel, "La mode, Qu'est que c'est?" *Coco Chanel Parle.*

8   Barry, "An Interview with Chanel," 170.

9   "Chanel, Chanel dit Non," *Marie-Claire* (France), March 1967, 62.

10 Coco Chanel, "Collections by Chanel," *McCall's*, August 1967.

11 "Chanel, Chanel dit Non," 62.

12 Marcel Haedrich, *Coco Chanel secrète* (Paris: Éditions Robert Laffont, 1971), 36–37.

13 Barry, "An Interview with Chanel," 170.

14 Haedrich, 61.

15 Haedrich, 20.

16 Haedrich, 32.

17 "Gabrielle Chanel," *Le Miroir du Monde*, May 12, 1934, no. 219, 44.

18 Barry, "An Interview with Chanel," 121.

19 Barry, "An Interview with Chanel," 170.

20 Paul Morand, *The Allure of Chanel*, trans. Euan Cameron (London: Pushkin Press, 2013), 13.

21 "Mlle Gabrielle Chanel" *Le Miroir du Monde*, November 4, 1933, 10.

22 Barry, "An Interview with Chanel," 170.

23 Barry, "An Interview with Chanel," 172.

24 Morand, 35.

25 Morand, 38.

26 Morand, 38–39.

27 Morand, 48.

28 Françoise Giroud, "La femme de la semaine: CHANEL," *L'Express*, August 17, 1956, 8.

29 Morand, 48.

30 Morand, 30.

31 Chanel, "La mode, Qu'est que c'est?" *Coco Chanel Parle.*

32 Morand, 47.

33 Chapsal, "Reportage Chanel au travail," 16.

34 Barry, "An Interview with Chanel," 170.

35 Barry, "An Interview with Chanel," 170.

36 Barry, "An Interview with Chanel," 170.

37 "Coco Chanel n'a eu qu'une robe longue dans sa vie," *Le Figaro*, February 25, 1969.

38 Barry, "An Interview with Chanel," 170.

39 James Brady, "Chanel," *WWD*, December 18, 1969, 10.

40 Brady, "Chanel," 10.

41 "Chanel, Chanel dit Non," 62.

42 "Chanel, Chanel dit Non," 62.

43 "Chanel, Chanel dit Non," 62.

44 "Chanel, Chanel dit Non," 62.

45 Berthod, "Qui était la vraie Chanel? Psychanalyse d'un monstre sacré," 33.

46 "Chanelorama," *Jours de France*, August 20, 1960, no. 301.

47 Barry, "An Interview With Chanel," 172.

48 "Mlle Chanel," *Marie-Claire* (France), September 1964, 65.

49 Morand, 51.

50 Marcel Zahar, "Faut-il poursuivre ou exploiter la copie," *Vu*, April 5, 1933, 510.

51 Paule Hutzler, "Comment nous faisons une parisienne cent pour cent," *Miroir du Monde*, April 8, 1933, 52.

52 Denise Weber, "LES PAGES Mademoiselle Chanel nous parle" *Marianne*, November 11, 1937.

53 Coco Chanel, "Collections by Chanel," *McCall's*, September 1967.

54 Chapsal, "Reportage Chanel au travail," 18.

55 "People," Time, July 12, 1963, 46.

56 Brady, "Chanel," 10.

57 Barry, "An Interview with Chanel," 170.

58 Giroud, ""La femme de la semaine : CHANEL," 8.

59 Chapsal, "Reportage Chanel au travail," 15.

60 Barry, "An Interview with Chanel," 168.

61 Zahar, "Faut-il poursuivre ou exploiter la copie," 510.

62 Morand, 112.

63 John Fairchild, "Viva Chanel," *Elle*, February 24, 1966, 72.

64 Chapsal, "Reportage Chanel au travail," 15.

65 Fairchild, "Viva Chanel," 72.

66 Patricia McColl, *WWD*, November 10, 1970.

67 "Eye to Eye," *WWD*, July 20, 1970, 10.

68 Noël, "She Twice Conquered Fashion World."

69 "G.C., Notre mode," *Le Témoin*, February 24, 1935.

70 G.Y. Dryansky, "Chanel Speaks," *WWD*, July 25, 1969, 8.

71 Weber, "LES PAGES Mademoiselle Chanel nous parle."

72 Noël, "She Twice Conquered Fashion World."

73 "En écoutant Chanel," *Elle* (France), August 23, 1963, 57.

74 "En écoutant Chanel," 57.

75 "En écoutant Chanel," 57.

76 Antoinette Nordmann, "Je ne suis qu'une petite couturière," *Elle* (France), September 9, 1957, 37.

77 Yves Salgues, "CHANEL," *Jours de France*, February 24, 1962, 41. N° 380

78 "Gabrielle Chanel, Jeunesse," *La Revue des Sports et du Monde*, Décembre, NOEL 1934, 33.

79 "Gabrielle Chanel, L'élégance et le Naturel," *La Revue des Sports et du Monde*, October 1934, 29.

80 "Gabrielle Chanel, Le cadeau de Noël de Coco Chanel, 14 conseils pour que vous restiez jeune," *Paris Match*, December 16, 1950, 51.

81 Barry, "An Interview with Chanel," 168.

82 "Chanel, Chanel dit Non," 62.

83 Fairchild, "Viva Chanel," 73.

84 McColl, *WWD*, November 10, 1970.

85 Barry, "An Interview with Chanel," 168.

86 "Gabrielle Chanel, Le cadeau de Noël de Coco Chanel, 14 conseils pour que vous restiez jeune," 51.

87 Barry, "An Interview with Chanel," 168.

88 "Le Paris des Parisiennes," *Marie-Claire* (France), October 1960, 13.

89 "Gabrielle Chanel, Le cadeau de Noël de Coco Chanel, 14 conseils pour que vous restiez jeune," 49.

90 Chapsal, "Reportage Chanel au travail," 16.

91 Nordmann, "Je ne suis qu'une petite couturière," 36.

92 Berthod, "Qui était la vraie Chanel? Psychanalyse d'un monstre sacré," 29.

93 Berthod, "Qui était la vraie Chanel? Psychanalyse d'un monstre sacré," 33.

94 Chanel, "Collections by Chanel," *McCall's* August 1967.

95 Chapsal, "Reportage Chanel au travail," 15.

96 Coco Chanel, "Collections by Chanel," *McCall's*, July 1967.

97 Chanel, "Collections by Chanel," *McCall's*, September 1967.

98 "Mlle Chanel," 65.

99 Morand, 165.

ELSA
SCHIAPARELLI

*Madame Schiaparelli, nothing in your background
indicates that you were predestined to work in fashion.*

I started by chance. I didn't know anything about materials and technicalities like the right bias, and cutting bored me. I never did a drawing in my life and I never had a designer. I chose the materials and I knew what I wanted. There were wonderful people working for me. I must have explained very clearly what I wanted because I usually got it.[1] I worked by instinct.[2]

Would you rather I called you "Schiap," which is how you invariably refer to yourself? You also have a habit of referring to yourself in the third person.

Schiap decidedly did not know anything about dressmaking. Her ignorance in this matter was supreme. Therefore her courage was without limit and blind. But what did she risk? She had no capital to speak of. She had no superiors. She did not have to report to anybody. The small freedom was hers. She learned then a few principles about clothes, principles made by herself, probably aided by surroundings of beauty she had in her childhood.[3]

Can you tell us about the difficulties you encountered when designing?

Dress designing, incidentally, is to me not a profession but an art. I found that it was a most difficult and unsatisfying art, because as soon as a dress is born it has already become a thing of the past. As often as not too many elements are required to allow one to realize the actual vision one had in mind. The interpretation of a dress, the means of making it, and the surprising way in which some materials react — all these factors, no matter how good an interpreter you have, invariably reserve a slight if not bitter disappointment for you. In a way it is even worse if you are satisfied, because once you have created it the dress no longer belongs to you. A dress cannot just hang like a painting on the wall, or like a book remain intact and live a long and sheltered life. A dress has no life of its own unless it is worn, and as soon as this happens another personality takes over from you and animates it, or tries to, glorifies or destroys it, or makes it into a song of beauty. More often it becomes an indifferent object, or even a pitiful caricature of what you wanted it to be — a dream, an expression.[4]

What is your conception of couture?

She felt that clothes had to be architectural: that the body must never be forgotten and it must be used as a frame is used in a building. The vagaries of lines and details or any asymmetric effect must always have a close connection with this frame.

The more the body is respected, the better the dress acquires vitality. One can add pads and bows, one can lower or raise the lines, modify the curves, accentuate this or that point, but the harmony must remain. The Greeks, more than anybody else except the Chinese, understood this rule, and gave to their goddesses, even when definitely fat, the serenity of perfection and the fabulous appearance of freedom.[5]

How do you see contemporary fashion?

This is a time of experiment. The outcome is still up in the air.[6]

Do you follow the work of other couturiers?

There are only two people whose clothes I look at now, Yves Saint Laurent and Courrèges. They are the only two who have any personality. I buy from both of them.[7]

Surely there are peers you admire?

Balenciaga. There's no doubt about it, then Vionnet and Chanel — she was a great girl and she achieved the incredible feat of doing the same thing for fifty years.[8]

You have gone on record as being quite critical of Paul Poiret.

Poiret wrote a book called *En habillant l'époque* (*On Dressing the Era*). It might be better to write a book called *En déshabillant les femmes* (*On Undressing Women*).[9]

How do you feel about young people's taste in fashion?

The young have come to a certain style of dressing which I call self-smartness. . . Both men and women choose what they feel is for them, from ready-made clothes they make what they want and sometimes it's good and sometimes it's bad. In a way they are being more inventive than the designers. The way they put things together shows imagination.[10]

What is the first rule of chic?

Wearing the right clothes in the right place at the right time is a rule of chic that is commonly violated.[11] When I last visited New York I was shocked to see women in mink coats buying pork chops. You *must* have a sense of the fitness of things, and you must give some intelligent consideration of the matter of where you're going to wear your clothes.[12] If you want to look smart, watch the clock. If you'll be out in the same costume through the afternoon and evening, wear something which is appropriate to both periods — a suit or a simple dress. You can change jewelry perhaps or other accessories to dress up your outfit as night falls. But most important of all: the chic woman is well-bred, well-spoken, well-groomed, and well-behaved![13]

Is there an ideal skirt length?

The real answer always depends on 'How good is the lady's leg'.[14]

How important is the dress that you choose to wear?

A woman is often striking, not by what she wears, but how she wears it.[15]

*How do fashions come into being,
and how do they become outdated?*

Sometimes one wonders how a fashion is born, or how a silhouette from another time can suddenly become fashionable again. There is one simple answer, which is popularity, and demand. There is also the manner in which one presents this creation, for the eye must habituate itself to a new form.[16]

Do you have a favorite clientele?

I find American women the easiest in the world to dress because they get so much fresh air and exercise.[17]

What makes them unique?

No woman in the world is more fashion-minded than the American woman, and has better opportunities to be well dressed on little money. . . Her greatest fault is that she buys too many things at a time. Buying clothes is like furnishing a house — you don't want to do it all at once.[18]

Are you inspired by America?

There is no question about it. America always inspires me. . .
Architecture is the greatest thing America has given the world
artistically, and I believe that, in due time, you will evolve a couture
of your own whose styles will bear the same stamp of originality
and beauty that your buildings have.[19]

Is there a special connection between fashion and cinema?

Cinema! What a wonderful way to launch a fashion! Much better
than the theater, where fashion only reaches a small amount of
people. The possibilities of the cinema are limitless. Only the
cinema can impose a form and directly influence taste.[20]

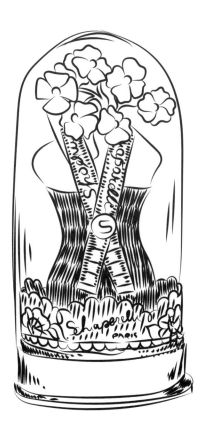

Could you tell us about your background?

My mother's mother was partly of Scottish origin (her father was
the English consul in Malta) and was brought up in the Far East.
At the age of twelve she married my grandfather, an Italian from
Salerno, and gave him five children, of whom my mother was the
youngest, before dying at the age of twenty. Her husband, at one time
a political exile, was imprisoned by the Bourbons, but escaped while
an uncle took his place in jail. . . My grandfather went to Egypt, took
up law, and became adviser to the khedive. . . My mother was then ten
and an orphan. She was tutored by a friend of the family, Count
Serristori, in Florence. My father came from the industrial district
of Piedmont. A sister of his became head of all the convents in Italy,
a brother became a famous astronomer.[21]

After having lived in Rome, London, and New York, in 1927
you settled in Paris, moving into an apartment situated at
20 rue de l'Université, which also became your first studio.
The furnishings were rather unusual, were they not?

Jean-Michel Franck made me an enormous couch in orange leather
and two low armchairs in green. The walls were white and the
curtains and chair covers were made of a white rubber substance that
was stiff and gleaming. The tables, like bridge tables, were black with
glass tops, the wall sofa chairs were in green rubber. There was really
nothing to it, but the whole thing was so new and unexpected that
it had charm. I gave my first dinner party, a formal one. Mademoiselle
Chanel came, and at the sight of this modern furniture and black
plates she shuddered as if she were passing a cemetery.[22]

There's a funny story about that dinner.
Can you share it with us?

With the heat of late spring (it was a very warm evening), the white
rubber on the chairs had transferred itself, unbeknownst to them,
to the dresses of the women and the trousers of the men, and when
dinner was over and they all got up, they looked like strange caricatures
of the sweaters that had paid for their meal![23]

*Indeed, sweaters marked your first foray into fashion.
How did that come about?*

The sweater my friend was wearing intrigued me. It was hand knitted and had what I might call a *steady* look. Many people have said and written that I started in business sitting in a window in Montmartre and knitting. In fact I hardly knew Montmartre and I have never been able to knit... "Where did you get it?" I asked. "A little woman..." The little woman turned out to be an Armenian peasant who lived with her husband... "If I make a design will you try to copy it?" I asked... So I drew a large butterfly bow in front, like a scarf round the neck — the primitive drawing of a child in prehistoric times. I said: "The bow must be white against a black ground, and there will be white underneath."[24]

Obviously the experiment turned out well.

I became very daring. The large bow was followed by gay woven handkerchiefs round the throat, by men's ties in gay colors, by hand-kerchiefs round the hops. Anita Loos, at the height of her career with *Gentlemen Prefer Blondes*, was my first private customer, and I was boosted, with her help, to fame.[25]

Did you yourself ever dare to wear a sweater in an elegant setting?

Trying courageously not to feel self-conscious, convinced deep within me that I was nearly glamorous, I wore it at a smart lunch — and created a furore. Women at that time were very sweater-minded. Chanel had, for quite a few years, made machine-knitted dresses and jumpers. This was different. All the women wanted one, immediately.[26] Soon the restaurant of the Ritz was filled with women from all over the world in black-and-white sweaters.[27]

What was so unique about them?

These sweaters were reinforced at the back with fine woolen stitching always in the same color as that of the contrasting figures. The stitches showed through discreetly, breaking the monotony of the background so that it gave an effect reminiscent of the impressionist school of painting.[28]

*Could you describe this crucial period that
became known as the Roaring Twenties?*

It was the time when abstract Dadaism and Futurism were the talk
of the world, the time when chairs looked like tables, and tables like
footstools, when it was not done to ask what a painting represented
or what a poem meant, when trifles of fantasy were taboo and only the
initiated knew about the Paris flea market, when women had no waists,
wore paste jewelry, and compressed their busts to look like boys.[29]

*In 1935, to celebrate the opening of your fashion house on Place
Vendôme, you decided to create a special fabric.*

That summer I took a trip . . . with a few friends. . . We crossed
Sweden by canal . . . and went to Copenhagen. There Schiap went one
day into the fish market, where old women . . . wore on their heads
newspapers twisted into queer shapes of hats. Schiap stood and
looked for a while. Back in Paris she sent for Colcombet, the most
daring of the textile men. "I want a material printed like a newspaper,"
she said. "But it will never sell!" exclaimed the terrorized man. "I
think it will," said Schiap. She clipped newspaper articles about
herself, both complimentary and otherwise, in every sort of language,
stuck them together like a puzzle, and had them printed on silk and
cotton. They came out in all kinds of colors and she turned them into
blouses, scarves, hats, and all kinds of bathing nonsense.[30]

*You also did something that was unheard of at the time: you opened
your own boutique on the ground floor of your fashion house.*

A new Schiap era came into being with the Place Vendôme. The year
1935 was such a busy one for Schiap that she wonders how she got
through it. To start with there was the birth of the boutique. The Schiap
boutique, the very first of its kind, has since been copied not only by
all the great Paris couturiers, but the idea has spread all over the world,
especially in Italy. It became instantaneously famous because of the
formula of "ready to be taken away immediately." There were useful
and amusing gadgets afire with youth. There were evening sweaters,
skirts, blouses, and accessories previously scorned by the haute couture.[31]

*In 1937 you produced the famous Shocking perfume, with
the racy bottle in the form of Mae West's curvaceous torso.*

Mae West came to Paris. She was stretched out on the operating table
of my workroom, and measured and probed with care and curiosity.
She had sent me all the most intimate details of her famous figure, and
for greater accuracy a plaster statue of herself quite naked in the pose
of the Venus de Milo.[32] From this silhouette also arose the bottle of
perfume shaped like a woman, that famous Schiaparelli perfume bottle
that practically became the signature of the house. Eleanore Fini
modeled it for me and the scent took more than a year to be ready.[33]

How did you come up with the famous Shocking color?

It remained for me to find a name for it and to choose in what color it should be presented. The name had to begin with an *S*, this being one of my superstitions. To find the name of a perfume is a very difficult problem because every word in the dictionary seems to be registered. The color flashed in front of my eyes. Bright, impossible, impudent, becoming, life-giving, like all the light and the birds and the fish in the world put together, a color of China and Peru but not of the West — a shocking color, pure and undiluted. So I called the perfume "Shocking." The presentation would be shocking, and most of the accessories and gowns would be shocking. It caused a mild panic amongst my friends and executives, who began to say that I was crazy ... The success was immense and immediate; the perfume, without advertising of any sort, took a leading place, and the color "shocking" established itself forever as a classic. Even Dali dyed an enormous stuffed bear in shocking pink and put drawers in its stomach.[34]

Presumably your taste for themed collections stems from that.

We worked hard but we had fun. The collections followed one another with definite themes. There was the pagan collection when women looked as if they had come out of a Botticelli painting, with wreaths and leaves of delicate flowers embroidered on simple, clinging classical gowns. There was an astrological collection with horoscopes, the stars, the moon, and the sun glittering at every step.

The most riotous and swaggering collection was that of the circus. Barnum, Bailey, Grock, and the Fratellinis got loose in a mad dance in the dignified showrooms, up and down the imposing staircase, in and out of the windows. Clowns, elephants, and horses decorated the prints with the words "Attention à la Peinture." Balloons for bags, spats for gloves, ice cream cones for hats, and trained Vasling dogs and mischievous monkeys ... The typical tempo of the time was marked by great enthusiasm. There was no criticism of "Who can wear it?" As an amazing fact, Schiap did not lose a single one of her wealthy conservative old-fashioned clients but got a lot of new ones — and of course, all the stars.[35]

Another innovation is your daring use of zippers.

Fashion even in the most difficult years, when it goes eccentric or foolish, undoubtedly retains some relation to politics. Schiap, catching the mood, showed regal clothes embroidered with pearls or daringly striped, but what upset the poor, breathless reporters most were the zips. Not only did they appear for the first time but in the most unexpected places, even on evening clothes. The whole collection was full of them. Astounded buyers bought and bought. They had come prepared for every kind of strange button. Indeed these had been the signature of the house.[36]

Tell us about those astonishing buttons.

In spite of the zippers, King Button still reigned without fear at Schiap's. The most incredible things were used, animals and feathers, caricatures and paperweights, chains, locks, clips, and lollipops. Some were of wood and others of plastic, but not one looked like what a button was supposed to look like. Along with these our own unusual jewelry of enameled ivy necklaces went like lightning, as did the first Plexiglas bracelets and earrings. They were designed by men of extraordinary talent. One of them was Jean Clément, a genius in his way, a real French artisan, who would work with such burning love that he was almost a fanatic. He would arrive at the last moment when we had given up all hope of having anything to fasten our clothes. There would be a smile of triumph on his face while he emptied his pockets into my lap, waiting anxiously for a word of praise. In his spare moments he would invent all kinds of strange machines — gadgets that we would put on our lapels and which would light up while we were out walking at night.[37]

Much has been said about your relationships
with certain famous artists.

Jean Cocteau made some drawings of heads for me. I reproduced
some of these on the back of an evening coat, and one, with long
yellow hair reaching to the waist, on a gray linen suit. I used to see
him often.[38] Aragon, the poet, with his wife, Elsa Triolet, author of
Les yeux d'Elsa, designed necklaces that looked like aspirins. The man
who does my buttons now is a grandnephew of Victor Hugo.[39] Dali
was a constant caller. We devised together the coat with many drawers
from one of his famous pictures. The black hat in the form of a shoe
with a Shocking velvet heel standing up like a small column was
another innovation . . . There was another hat resembling a lamb
cutlet with a white frill on the bone, and this, more than anything
else, contributed to Schiap's fame for eccentricity.[40]

What else did you get out of these collaborations?

Artists took much more part in the life and development of
fashion than they do now. The magazines encouraged us and
sought our help and advice. As I look back through prewar
magazines I am astounded by the difference. The presentation
of fashion was a work of art, a truly beautiful thing, and a great
deal of importance was attached to genuine creation. At that
time it was not a matter of pure advertising interests: of who
bought and how widely a model could be reproduced.

The present system tends to produce dullness and
it often gives a very one-sided idea of what is going on. Working
with artists like Bébé Bérard, Jean Cocteau, Salvador Dalí, Vertès,
van Dongen; and with photographers like Honingen-Huni [sic],
Horst, Cecil Beaton, and Man Ray gave one a sense of exhilaration.
One felt supported and understood beyond the crude and boring
reality of merely making a dress to sell.[41]

You decided to keep your fashion house
open during World War II.

As we expected a quick and savage bombardment, most of the
employees had to be evacuated; but when no bombardment came and
we went round town with our useless gas-masks, some forgetting
them in taxis, others using them as handbags or hiding bottles of
whiskey or gin in them, thinking that in the event of an alarm a stiff
drink would be more reviving than gas, Schiap called her dispersed
staff together to ask them if they would like to take the risk of coming
back to work, though at lower wages because of the lack of business.
They readily and graciously accepted part-time work. Thus business
began again in a small way.[42]

I wonder if people fully realized the importance as propaganda
for France of the dressmaking business at this time. The opposition of
feminine grace to cruelty and hate reached farther than plays or books.
From six hundred employees we came down to one hundred and fifty.
The little black school desks at which my salesgirls sat at the entrance
were half empty! Some of the midinettes had to walk twelve miles to
come to work. We built up a collection in three weeks hoping for some
response. This was the "cash and carry" collection with huge pockets
everywhere so that a woman, obliged to leave home in a hurry or to
go on duty without a bag, could pack all that was necessary to her.
She could thus retain the freedom of her hands and yet manage to look
feminine. There was an evening dress camouflaged to look like a day
dress. When one emerged from the subway at night to attend a formal
dinner, one merely pulled a ribbon and the day dress was lengthened
into an evening dress. There were the Maginot Line blue, the Foreign
Legion red, the airplane gray, the woolen boiler suit that one could fold
on a chair next to one's bed so that one could put it on quickly in the
event of an air-raid driving one down to the cellar. There was also one
in white which was supposed to withstand poisonous gas.[43]

What difficulties did you face?

Right from the beginning of the war, of course, great difficulties confronted the *couture* in France. All branches of the industry were affected, and everything was upset. We could count on nothing. The accessories were immediately hit, with leather and metals for buttons and bags taken for the army. Silks, some of them were taken for airplane cloth. . . Certain dyes, especially some yellows, were proscribed. Rapidly, we learned to do without all these things, however; to depend more and more on personal struggle and on the tricks of our own invention.[44]

Could you share some examples with us?

Because of the lack of buttons and safety-pins there were dog chains to close suits and to hold skirts. Maurice Chevalier's latest song was printed on one scarf, the restrictions which Parisians endured on another. Thus: "Monday — no meat. Tuesday — no alcohol. Wednesday — no butter. Thursday — no fish. Friday — no meat. Saturday — no alcohol . . . but Sunday — *toujours l'amour.*" The tweed skirts were split on the side to go bicycling, thus revealing gaily printed bloomers to match the blouse. So the *grande couture* carried on, filling the hours, the minutes, and the seconds with work and humor to prevent the soul from sinking in despair.[45] The shortage was not only in materials but in work people, for men were not back from prison camps and deportation, and homes were still disrupted. Our mannequins were so ill fed that they were too thin. No woolen coat could be lined with wool, there was no fur at all, no dress could have more than three yards of material, and only sixty models were allowed to be shown at a collection.[46]

In 1942 you traveled to New York and organized
the exhibition First Papers of Surrealism.

In order to deal with the present and the future, I thought it would be interesting to have a show completely modern and d'avant garde. I asked Marcel Duchamp, who had startled the artistic world with his famous painting of a naked woman descending a staircase, to help me organize it.

Marcel is a very special case. He gave in his paintings, in short staccato sentences, the most perfect definition of surrealism, left it when he thought he had said all he had to say, started playing chess, and became a champion. He promised me his collaboration, and painfully emerging from his solitude set to work with astounding results. The lofty rooms were divided by screens for hanging purposes, and between them ropes were stretched to form a labyrinth directing the visitors to this and that painting with a definite sense of contrast. On the opening day small children played with balloons between the legs of the rather bewildered crowd. It was an amazing collection of pictures. The most famous modern artists were represented and many, like the Picassos dating from 1937 to 1938, had not been shown before in America.[47]

How popular are you?

A short time ago, a poll was taken at the corner of Forty-second Street and Fifth Avenue in New York, to discover from passersby which French name was best known to them, and — to my pleasure and utter surprise — mine came first.[48]

You returned to Paris after the war. When did you
sense that a real change had taken place?

This brings me to 1947, the tolling of the bell, when the New Look, cleverly planned and magnificently financed, achieved, to the greatest din of publicity ever known, the shortest life of any fashion in history.[49]

Why did you decide to close your house in 1954?

Because women cannot afford to pay the fabulous prices we are compelled to ask.[50]

*Any professional advice you would care to share
with our female readership?*

These things you ought to bear in mind always: buy *good* things
only and never be afraid of wearing them too often or of not "being
in style." If you have good clothes, in good taste, you will always be
chic and you can ignore passing fads.[51] Don't be afraid of being
conspicuous if you've chosen clothes which look good on you.[52]

Easier said than done.

No woman can ever get an entirely objective slant on herself
without critical outside help . . . Seek outside help on matters
of grooming, and get an expert's opinion whenever you can.[53]

How should one choose one's wardrobe?

Whether you are trying to crash the gates of Hollywood, or to make
a smart impression upon your sweetheart, or merely wish to be chic
at all times, these suggestions will apply to you. . . Begin building your
wardrobe with a good suit and add to it as you can afford it, a good
coat, two plain dresses for afternoon or dinner, a smart evening dress
which will do duty winter and summer, and an evening wrap. For the
first dress, I would suggest a good crepe with two different scarves to
be worn with a black coat with a fur collar. In the case of the evening
dress, add a little jacket for informal parties, and leave it off for the
formals. For winter, you should have a three-quarter fur coat,
or if you cannot afford fur, a heavy tweed.[54]

How important are accessories?

Shoes, hats, bag, and gloves are frightfully important and should
be considered together. All should match in color. . . You should
have a minimum of two hats, one a felt to wear with oxfords and
a sport blouse; with the same suit a dressy blouse, a dressy hat,
and pumps and you can go anywhere in the afternoon.[55] As to shoes,
you should have a minimum of one pair of oxfords, one pair of
pumps with Cuban heels, and one pair of evening sandals in either
silver or gold (they last a long time).

Shoes should never be conspicuous. Don't wear "fussy" shoes with trimming, bows, perforations, etc. A shoe, to be really smart, should be as plain as possible with a heel that suits the girl who wears it. . . Feet are sometimes so over-dressed that you can't tell what else their owner is wearing.[56]

How about handbags?

It's better to own one good bag than half a dozen of inferior quality.[57]

With or without jewelry?

Pearls, including cheap imitations, are always in good taste. Plain gold jewelry in a modern design is always good. Avoid long earrings except for eveningwear and shun cheap beads as you would the plague. Generally speaking, keep *simple*.[58]

Why is it important to accent the upper body?

By drawing attention to the shoulders we get that fine slenderness that suggests the Egyptian ideal of beauty.[59]

How would you sum up your unusual career?

Two words have always been banned from my house — the word *creation*, which strikes me as the height of pretentiousness, and the word *impossible*.[60]

NOTES

1 Anne Head, "The Sloppy Seventies," *The Observer*, July 25, 1971, 25.

2 Untitled article, *Chicago Tribune*, October 11, 1971, C12.

3 Elsa Schiaparelli, *Shocking Life* (London: J. M. Dent & Sons, 1954), 50.

4 Schiaparelli, 46.

5 Schiaparelli, 50–51.

6 Angela Cuccio, "Elsa," *The Washington Post*, July 6, 1969.

7 Head, "The Sloppy Seventies," 25.

8 Head, "The Sloppy Seventies," 25.

9 Schiaparelli, 58.

10 Cuccio, "Elsa."

11 Sylvia Blythe, "Mirrors Can Lie," *The Atlantic Constitution*, February 18, 1940, A14.

12 Elsa Schiaparelli as told to Harold S. Kahm, "How to Be Chic on a Small Income," *Photoplay*, August 1936, 60.

13 Ormond Gigli, "A Woman Chic," *The Los Angeles Times*, May 8, 1955, K9.

14 "Skirt Lengths Depend on Leg—Schiaparelli," *The Atlanta Constitution*, November 11, 1941, 7.

15 Gigli, "A Woman Chic."

16 J.F. "Le Cinéma influence-t-il la Mode?" *Le Figaro Illustré*, February 1933, 80.

17 Kahm, "How to Be Chic on a Small Income."

18 Gigli, "A Woman Chic," K9.

19 "Schiaparelli Gives Ideas on Fashions," *The China Press*, April 12, 1933, 17.

20 Emma Cabire, "Le Cinéma & La Mode," *La revue du cinéma*, September 1, 1931, 24.

21 Schiaparelli, 3–4.

22 Schiaparelli, 53.

23 Schiaparelli, 53.

24 Schiaparelli, 47.

25 Schiaparelli, 48–49.

26 Schiaparelli, 48.

27 Schiaparelli, 49.

28 Schiaparelli, 49.

29 Schiaparelli, 49.

30 Schiaparelli, 73–74.

31 Schiaparelli, 70–71.

32 Schiaparelli, 95.

33 Schiaparelli, 96.

34 Schiaparelli, 96–97.

35 Schiaparelli, 99.

36 Schiaparelli, 72.

37 Schiaparelli, 98.

38 Schiaparelli, 98.

39 Schiaparelli, 9–99.

40 Schiaparelli, 97–98.

41 Schiaparelli, 75.

42 Schiaparelli, 110–11.

43 Schiaparelli, 113–14.

44 Elsa Schiaparelli, "Needles and Guns,"
    Vogue, September 1940, 57.

45 Schiaparelli, 115.

46 Schiaparelli, 174.

47 Schiaparelli, 167.

48 Schiaparelli, 184.

49 Schiaparelli, 186.

50 Henry Wales, "Elsa Schiaparelli to
    Quit Designing Expensive Dresses,"
    Chicago Daily Tribune, March 12, 1954, B7.

51 Kahm, "How to Be Chic
    on a Small Income."

52 Gigli, "A Woman Chic."

53 Blythe, "Mirrors Can Lie."

54 Kahm, "How to Be Chic
    on a Small Income," 60.

55 Kahm, "How to Be Chic
    on a Small Income."

56 Kahm, "How to Be Chic
    on a Small Income."

57 Gigli, "A Woman Chic."

58 Kahm, "How to Be Chic
    on a Small Income."

59 Linda Greenhouse, "Schiaparelli
    Dies in Paris; Brought Color to
    Fashion," *The New York Times*,
    November 15, 1973, 93.

60 Schiaparelli, 56.

CRISTÓBAL BALENCIAGA

The very soul of discretion, Spanish designer Cristóbal Balenciaga is known as the "Garbo of the Paris couture."[1] Given that his lone interview to the press dates from a few months before his death, I have called upon seven of his contemporaries in the hope of gaining a better understanding of the man "we all call [Cristóbal] 'seigneur,'"[2] and of whom it has been said, "If any person is sacred to fashion it's King Cristóbal Balenciaga."[3]

Gathered here we have Cecil Beaton (celebrated portraitist, fashion photographer, set designer, costume maker, and writer), Bettina Ballard (fashion editor of *Vogue*), John Fairchild (publisher and editor of *Women's Wear Daily*), Prudence Glynn (journalist at *The Times*), Carmel Snow (editor-in-chief of *Harper's Bazaar*), Diana Vreeland (fashion editor of *Harper's Bazaar*, editor-in-chief of *Vogue,* and consultant to the Costume Institute of the Metropolitan Museum of Art), and last but not least, the inexorable Coco Chanel.

> *Sir Cecil Beaton, how important was Balenciaga to the world of fashion?*

In the world of present-day dressmakers, Balenciaga stands apart, like some Elizabethan malcontent meditating upon the foibles and follies of fashion, yet committed to acting and creating in the very world which he regards with a classical Spanish eye. He is so much the opposite of a Christian Dior that they might well be placed at the far ends of the dressmaking world; yet each has a respect for the work of the other, and each is unquestionably a genius of contemporary style. If Dior is the Watteau of dressmaking — full of nuances, chic, delicate, and timely — then Balenciaga is fashion's Picasso. For like that painter, underneath all his experiments with the modern, Balenciaga has a deep respect for tradition and a pure classic line.[4]

In his work Balenciaga shows the refinement of France and the strength of Spain. His dresses have elegance and solidity; like their maker they can mingle with kings and keep the common touch. . . Balenciaga uses fabrics like a sculptor working on marble. He can rip a suit apart with his thumbs and remake or alter his vision in terms of practical, at-hand dressmaking. It is even possible that he makes no sketches at all, relying entirely on the picture in his mind.[5] Balenciaga's color sense is so refined, sharpened to such a remarkable degree, that he can unerringly scan four hundred colors and choose the right one for his purpose.[6]

If one looks at the art of dressmaking and strips it to its essentials, considering it in its simplest terms, then one must concede that Balenciaga is indeed today's Titan among couturiers.[7]

*Please tell us, John Fairchild,
how Balenciaga began his career.*

He started at thirteen in Guetaria, a thirteenth-century Spanish fishing village, where his father was a sea captain and his mother sewed for wealthy summer residents. It was at this time that Cristóbal, still studying, took a job with Galerias El Louvre, the first department-store type shop in San Sebastián.[8] Balenciaga opened his Paris house in 1937, 10 avenue George-V, leaving Spain during the Spanish Civil War. He built a fashion monastery where elegant women and the world's buyers go "not to see a collection, but to worship in Balenciaga's church," says couturier Antonio del Castillo.[9]

How would you describe him, Bettina Ballard?

Cristóbal Balenciaga, when I first met him with André Durst
in Paris in 1937, was a gentle-voiced Spaniard with fine pale skin
the texture and color of eggshells and dark hair that lay thick and
glistening in wavy layers on his well-shaped head. His voice was like
feathers, and his intimate, quick smile had never been used to express
anything but true pleasure, which gave his face a guileless quality.
His instinctive, spontaneous charm was completely untutored —
a charm that has inspired devotion from everyone who has known
or worked with him through the years.[10] I remember once when
the press had stomped on the floor and yelled "bravo" until they
were hoarse, out of unprecedented enthusiasm for a great collection,
and I had gone back to his studio to see him, only to find him in his
white working blouse tearing apart the seams of one of the suits he
had just shown. "It's not right — it's never right the first time," he said.
He was deaf to the cheers, blank with fatigue — only the momentum
of work carried him on.[11]

Any thoughts, Madame Snow?

When I began buying most of my clothes from Balenciaga, he often
had me fitted in his apartment, fussing endlessly until they entirely
pleased him, often suggesting changes in color . . . For Balenciaga's
work is his life, except for his family and the few people he admits
to his friendship.[12]

*Mademoiselle Chanel, I have it on good authority that
you once knew Cristóbal Balenciaga very well.*

The other day, I was talking to my good friend Balenciaga, whom
I love and admire. "Cristóbal," I said, "take care. You have a style
of your own. Keep to it. That is what they come to you for — the
Balenciaga style — just as they come to me for my suits. Your lines are
stark and simple and elegant. Your style demands this. So, Cristóbal,
fais attention, take care and remain yourself — and use only the best
of everything in style, fabrics, and colors."[13]

*Would you care to add anything about Balenciaga
and Chanel's friendship, Mr. Fairchild?*

Balenciaga and Chanel had been close friends. It made a picture,
better than anything in fashion, Balenciaga and Chanel walking
together in the Zurich woods. But those days together in Swiss
peace and security ended abruptly. Waspish Chanel stung her
sensitive friend and rival Balenciaga by an off-the-cuff remark
to a French newspaper reporter and when he saw her words
in print, the King promptly ordered his secretary to wrap all
Chanel's gifts and send them back.[14]

Monsieur Beaton, what do you see as Balenciaga's legacy?

Proud, Spanish, classical, he is a strange rock to be found in the
middle of the changing sea of fashion, and one which will endure
long after the capricious waves of the moment have done their
best to dislodge him.[15]

Anything you would care to add, John Fairchild?

Balenciaga is the father of disciplined, understated, chic clothes.[16]

*Mrs. Vreeland, you curated a Balenciaga retrospective
at the Metropolitan Museum of Art. What would you
say he brought to fashion?*

Balenciaga brought the body and dress together in harmony and
suddenly a woman found herself in perfect rhythm with the universe.
She found herself in delectable colors and combinations and almost
impossible perfection. He loved the coquetry of lace and ribbon,
of floating taffeta and racy day clothes cut with such gusto and flair
of tailoring as the Western world has never known.[17]

*Prudence Glynn, as the only journalist ever to have had
the privilege of interviewing Señor Balenciaga, what
surprised you most about him?*

The one thing I had never imagined this great austere figure
to be was funny, but he is and his eyes twinkle with spirit.[18]

*And so, Monsieur Balenciaga, I am pleased
to let you have the last word.*

When I was a young man I was told by a specialist that I could never
pursue my chosen *métier* of couturier because I was far too delicate.
Nobody knows what a hard *métier* it is, how killing is the work.
Under all this luxury and glamour . . . *c'est la vie d'un chien.*[19]

⸱ NOTES ⸱

1   John Fairchild, *The Fashionable Savages* (New York: Doubleday, 1965), 47.

2   No author, "Dictator by Demand," *Time*, March 4, 1957.

3   Fairchild, 45.

4   Cecil Beaton, *The Glass of Fashion* (New York: Doubleday, 1954), 304.

5   Beaton, 308.

6   Beaton, 314.

7   Beaton, 309.

8   Fairchild, 45.

9   Fairchild, 46.

10   Bettina Ballard, *In My Fashion* (New York: Secker & Warburg, 1960), 109.

11   Ballard, 110.

12   Carmel Snow with Mary Louise Aswell, *The World of Carmel Snow* (New York: McGraw-Hill, 1962), 166.

13   Lucie Noël, "She Twice Conquered Fashion World," *The Herald Tribune*, August 4, 1960.

14   Fairchild, 45.

15   Beaton, 314.

16   Fairchild, 46.

17   Diana Vreeland, "Balenciaga: An Appreciation," in *The World of Balenciaga* (New York: The Metropolitan Museum of Art, 1973), 9.

18   Prudence Glynn, "Balenciaga and la vie d'un chien," *The Times*, August 3, 1971.

19   Glynn, "Balenciaga and la vie d'un chien."

CHRISTIAN DIOR

*Monsieur Dior, what kind of life does
a famous man such as yourself lead?*

My life is limited to the preparation of a collection, and the
torments, joys, and disappointments that go along with it.[1]

*You make a clear distinction between Christian Dior
the man, who remains very attached to his roots, and
your alter ego, the world-famous fashion designer.*

There is Christian Dior, the man in the public eye, and Christian Dior,
the private individual — who seem to get further and further apart. One
thing is certain: I was born at Granville in Normandy on January 21, 1905,
to Alexandre Louis Maurice Dior, manufacturer, and Madeleine Martin,
housewife. Half-Parisian and half-Norman, I am still attached to my native
Normandy, though I rarely go there now. I like small intimate gatherings
of old friends; I detest the noise and bustle of the world and sudden, violent
changes. The one [you're concerned with] is the dress designer. Ensconced
in a magnificent group of buildings on the avenue Montaigne, he is a
compound of people, dresses, hats, furs, stockings, perfumes, publicity
notices, press photographs, and, every now and then, a small bloodless
revolution — made by the scissors rather than the sword — whose rever-
berations extend to all corners of the world.[2] My fellow countryman
Gustave Flaubert defended one of the characters in a novel of his before
a court with the bold words: "*I* am Madame Bovary." And were Christian
Dior, couturier, ever to involve me in a similar situation, I should
certainly defend him with my last breath: "I am he!" For whether I like
it or not, my inmost hopes and dreams are expressed in his creations.[3]

How does that work?

Sometimes I get the impression that another Christian Dior is
talking, walking, and going about his business. When that happens
I stop what I'm doing and take a long, hard look at myself. I suppose
one could say that I have a split personality.[4]

*In Normandy when you were a teenager, a fortuneteller gave you
some insight into your future. What exactly did she tell you?*

You will be poor, but you will achieve success through women. You
will make a great deal of money out of them, and will have to travel
widely. The ambiguous phrase, "You will make a great deal of money
out of women" has since been fully explained, but at the time it must
have mystified my parents as much as it did me.[5]

You ran an art gallery for a while.

I had the good fortune to know painters and musicians (Bérard, Dalí, Sauguet, Poulenc, especially), with whom I was on very friendly terms, and I was so pleased with their successes that it never occurred to me to want to do anything myself. To admire and to have my friends was enough to keep me happy.[6]

How did you start out in fashion?

I was living in Paris with a friend of mine, Jean Ozenne, who at that time was designing model gowns and hats. To cheer me up a little he suggested that I should do the same, and thus it was that I began, rather tremulously, guided by him and by Max Kenna, to make my first sketches. Mixed among his own, my sketches were subjected to the scrutiny of a *maison de couture* and, to my great surprise, they were immediately bought. Encouraged by the first success, I went on in this career without very much reflection. With the admirable presumption of ignorance, making use of magazines and tracing silhouettes from them, I undertook to design a collection. And this, by a miracle, was sold.[7] It was then that I began to find out all that was entailed in this profession to which I aspired: the long waits in the anterooms of fashion houses or in the halls of large hotels; urgent appointments. This hard school was to prove of great service to me.[8]

In 1938 Robert Piguet hired you as a design assistant.

This was the chance I had been waiting for. At last I had got into the workshop! I accepted with enthusiasm. Everything leads me to believe that I was not too unsuccessful with the first collection, because by it my position with that house was established.[9] I have happy memories of the years spent with Robert Piguet. If, now and then, the firm was troubled by certain little intrigues (which I must confess, gave great amusement to my beloved *patron*, and which he used to take a little malicious pleasure in stirring up), at least the arguments were always carried on with perfect courtesy.[10]

What did your time with him teach you?

I learned to "omit." This is very important. The very technique of dressmaking was deliberately simplified there. . . But Piguet knew that elegance can be found only in simplicity, and this he taught me to understand. I owe him very much, and above all I owe him the confidence which I gained in myself at a time when I did not have very much experience.[11]

In 1941 you began working for Lucien Lelong.

In this large fashion house, with its numerous staff and immense premises, I shared with Pierre Balmain the responsibilities of designing. I think that, as the result of his charming disposition — and also mine! — there is no example in the history of dressmaking of a more complete understanding between two designers. After all, fashions are created above everything by emulation, if not by rivalry. We found a way of avoiding intrigues and jealousy, our first care being the success of the collections. But Balmain saw in this work only a stepping-stone. He was already dreaming of the house which he would himself found and which one day would bear his name. He also encouraged me to dream my own dreams. Often he would say to me, "Christian Dior is a good name for a fashion house!"[12]

How did Piguet and Lelong differ in their approaches?

If Robert Piguet could be said to represent the very spirit of elegance, Lucien Lelong for his part represented a tradition. He did not design himself, but worked through his designers. Nevertheless, in the course of his career as couturier his collections retained a style which was really his own and greatly resembled him. It was while I was with Lucien Lelong that, as I familiarized myself with the trade, I learned the importance of this principle — the most essential one in dress-making: *the direction of a material*. With the same idea and the same material, a dress may be a success or a complete failure, depending on whether or not one has known how to direct the natural move-ment of the cloth, which one must always obey.[13]

Which designers did you admire at the time?

If I think back to that moment and try to analyze or to define
my views on fashion and the ideas I may have had of elegance,
two names immediately come to mind: Chanel and Molyneux.[14]
Mainbocher dresses I also found very beautiful, but as I have already
said, my preference was for Molyneux. Nothing is ever invented,
everything springs from something else. His is certainly the style
which has most influenced me. Finally, in 1938, the star of Balenciaga,
for whose talent I have a very high admiration, rose up in triumph.
Madame Grès, under the name of Alix, had just opened her house,
in which every single dress was a masterpiece. Dress designing owes
a great deal to those two designers of genius. I must also mention
two women whom I never met, because their houses had already
disappeared at the time when I was beginning. Everything of theirs
I have ever seen has seemed the very summit of taste and perfection in
la grande couture. They are Augusta Bernard and Louise Boulanger.[15]

What about Mademoiselle Chanel?

Mademoiselle Chanel was one of the most intelligent and brilliant
women in all Paris. I greatly admired her. Her elegance, even to an
ignoramus, was dazzling. With a black pullover and ten rows of pearls
she revolutionized the world of fashion . . . Her personal style was
characteristic of her era: by creating a style for the elegant woman
rather than the beautiful woman she marked the end of froufrou,
feathers, overdressing.[16]

How do you feel about Madeleine Vionnet's work?

I must admit that her dresses interested me above all when I was
myself becoming a dress designer and was preoccupied with problems
of technique. The more I learned of my art, the better I understood
how admirable and exceptional her dresses are. Never has the art
of the dress designer reached greater heights.[17]

And Elsa Schiaparelli?

If I consider dressmaking as a whole, as it was then, that is to say in the period just before World War II, I see above everything else the triumph of the style and imagination of Schiaparelli, which I will not attempt to assess here; but it was the *mode*, it stood for elegance, and for an elegance which accorded very well with the decorations of Jean-Michel Franck and the extravagance of surrealism . . .[18]

> *The period between World War I and World War II*
> *was particularly innovative.*

Paul Poiret changed everything. Whereas *toilettes* used to be as fastidiously detailed as medieval illuminated manuscripts, he came up with exciting models with surprising colors, executed with a few inspired snips of the scissors. Madeleine Vionnet, Jeanne Lanvin, Mademoiselle Chanel — they all asserted the primary importance of the cut. This genuine revolution led us to where we are today. If a dressmaker can talk today about his métier, it's because he is now an artist in his own right, and not a mere craftsman. He signs his dresses, because he wants to set his own sartorial standard. Style now takes precedence over fabric.[19]

It was Madeleine Vionnet and Jeanne Lanvin who truly transformed the dressmaking profession by executing the dresses in their collections with their own hands and scissors. The model became a whole and at last skirt and bodice were cut according to the same principle. Vionnet achieved wonders in this direction, she was a genius at using her material, and she invented the famous bias cut which gave women's clothes of the period between the two wars their softly molded look. Dresses now depended on their cut. That was the era of the great couturiers. Outstanding among them was Mademoiselle Chanel, who dominated all the rest although she prided herself on being unable to sew a stitch. Her personality as well as her taste had style, elegance, and authority. From quite different points of view, she and Madeleine Vionnet can claim to be the creators of modern fashion.[20]

You appeared on the scene in 1946.

I was designing dresses for Lucien Lelong, and was making a nice living; I had a charming profession and was free of all the responsibilities that go along with being the boss; I also didn't have to worry about the commercial aspects of the business. In short, it was truly a delightful existence.[21] Thus, with one collection after another causing one regret after the other at not having been able to do what was in my heart, I came to the conclusion that, to do so, I should have to have my hands free. Chance having brought me into touch with Monsieur Boussac, a whole chain of circumstances finally led me to assume the responsibility of a business under my own name.[22]

Tell us how this came about.

I met my fate while walking from rue Saint-Florentin to rue Royale, where I lived in a one-bedroom apartment. Naturally, my fortuneteller had predicted it. Fate appeared to me in the form of a childhood friend with whom I had played long ago on the beach at Granville, and whom I had not seen for many long years. He was now a director of Gaston, a dressmaking house on rue Saint-Florentin, and he knew that I had become a designer. He told me that Monsieur Boussac, the owner of the House of Gaston, wanted to reorganize the whole house drastically, and was looking for a designer capable of infusing new life into it.[23]

How did you respond?

I thought for a few moments before telling him that regretfully I could think of no one who could possibly fit that description.[24]

What happened next?

Fate (and my fortuneteller) were quite stubborn. I ran into my old friend a second time, on the same stretch of sidewalk. He was still looking, and I was still unable to believe for a second that I could be the person he was looking for.[25]

But you finally seized the occasion.

I wondered whether I was really devoid of personal ambition.
When fate brought me face to face with my friend for the third time,
at the same place, my mind was made up. Without realizing for a
moment that I was altering the whole course of my life, I said boldly,
"Well, what about me?" I made a quick stop at my fortuneteller's,
and she said, "It has to be you." The die was cast. And yet, the idea
of meeting Monsieur Boussac, head of the Cotton Industry Board,
seemed an insurmountable obstacle to someone as shy as I. And the
word *business*, with its sinister implications, had always terrified me.[26]

How did your meeting with Monsieur Boussac go?

Shy people can sometimes have bursts of sudden eloquence.
A mysterious force took over — I wondered if my fortuneteller
was talking in my stead — and I heard myself say that instead of
breathing new life into the House of Gaston, I wanted to create
a new fashion establishment under my own name, in a district
of my own choosing.[27]

> *You reached an agreement with Monsieur Boussac,*
> *and everything was set in motion. You just needed*
> *to decide on a location.*

The fashion house of my dreams would be small and secluded,
with very few workrooms, but within those rooms the work
would be done according to the highest standards of dressmaking,
for a clientele of extremely fashionable women. The designs, for
all their simplicity, would, in fact, involve elaborate workmanship
. . . I was determined to get the one that suited me. It turned out
that many years before that decisive life-changing interview with
him, I had in fact stopped short in front of two small houses side
by side on avenue Montaigne — numbers 28 and 30.[28]

A rather funny thing happened when you set out to hire your models, or mannequins, *as they were called in your day.*

It is never particularly easy to find the right mannequins, and I chose a peculiarly unfortunate time to try. In despair at not being able to find the type of girl I wanted, I decided to put an advertisement in the paper. As luck would have it, I chose the exact moment when a new law was forcing certain Paris "houses" to close down, and many of their former occupants found themselves without regular employment. These ladies read my advertisement and were overjoyed; perhaps they imagined that a dressmaking establishment opening discreetly in a modest house in the avenue Montaigne must surely serve as a front for some more disreputable trade! On the appointed day, my house, where work was already under way, was literally invaded by cohorts of the most unmistakable kind. Madame Raymonde, who had the job of screening the applicants, was terrified, and wondered what on earth to do with them. I decided I must see the whole lot. From Toulouse-Lautrec's type downward, I found myself interviewing every unemployed good-time girl in Paris; several of them were actually very pretty, but none of them had the sort of looks suited to my purpose. After all, a dress designer can't forget that the first fashion magazine was named *Le Bon Genre* (*The Proper Thing*).[29]

And then the great day of your first show finally arrived, February 12, 1947.

Thus we have come to the beginnings of the house of Christian Dior. What can I tell you of my house? How can I speak of the present and of what is happening now? My firm is, in fact, the whole of my life. I can, however, confess that on the eve of the first collection, the one which introduced the "New Look," if I had been asked what I had done and what I hoped from it, I should certainly not have spoken of "revolution." I could not foresee the reception that it was to have, so little had I conceived such a thing possible, all my efforts having been directed toward giving of my best.[30]

*After your first show, Carmel Snow, editor in chief
of* Harper's Bazaar, *praised your collection. To describe
it, she coined the term "New Look," a title of glory that
became known the world over.*

The style that was universally hailed as new and original was nothing
but the sincere and natural expression of a fashion I had always
sought to achieve. It happened that my own inclinations coincided
with the spirit or sensibility of the times.[31]

*How were your designs different from those
that had been prevalent until then?*

As a result of wartime uniforms, women still looked and dressed like
Amazons. But I designed clothes for flowerlike women, clothes with
rounded shoulders, full feminine busts, and willowy waists above
enormous spreading skirts.[32]

How do you start off working on a collection?

One of the strangest aspects of the designer's profession is that fashion is always decided out of season: the winter collection is worked upon in the season of lilacs and cherry blossoms, the summer collection when the leaves or the first snowflakes are falling. Yet, oddly enough, the distance separating the creator from the season for which he is designing is an advantage of sorts. It allows him to introduce a nostalgic note, the added inspiration of hunger for the sun or for fog. A few weeks earlier, the designer prepared or chose his designs — sometimes in the hundreds. And yet they are all somewhat similar. Naturally, every designer finds inspiration in his own way. But one shouldn't believe that these multitudinous documents necessarily give birth to a new silhouette. Most of the time, that happens fortuitously. The more you design dresses, the more you see them — even where they are not. All of a sudden, in a flash, a sketch reveals its nature. That's the one! Imagine you're waiting for friends at the train station. People are getting off the train, anonymous, slow, disappointing since they are never the ones you are hoping to see. Then all of a sudden your friend appears! It's the same for the key sketches: it is impossible not to recognize it when it appears. Once you have it, things become intense. You create variations on its theme. Now you are sketching with growing confidence. And then, the next day, or even that night, another silhouette emerges from the crowd, another friend you immediately recognize. You open your arms wide for a hug. These sketches, which are similar to long-lost friends, are going to lead you down the road to the new fashion.[33]

Once the silhouette is found, it needs to take shape.
How important is the material?

Most of my fabrics spring naturally from the inventiveness of a technician who knows how to foresee what I want or how to challenge me. Fabric not only expresses a designer's dreams but also stimulates his own ideas. It can be the beginning of an inspiration. Many a dress of mine is born of the fabric alone.[34]

Thus the atmosphere of the collection starts to be formed. Suddenly one is plunged in the middle of an ocean of materials, each more marvelous than the last, and which one is dying to use. This is the moment when one must be able to resist temptations and avoid the traps of too beautiful a material, which its very beauty sometimes makes it impossible to use. Imperceptibly the elimination is made, the final choice decided on, and one starts to think of dresses.[35]

Tell us about the next phase.

A dress does not spring from a mere drawing. The drawing is but
a sketch. Once Madame Marguerite has distributed my drawings
to the workshops, the *toiles*, or muslin models, start coming my way,
and then I begin creating my dresses. The collection starts taking
shape during the last three weeks, though it represents three months'
work.[36] After the first models have been fitted and finally decided
on, the rest of the collection seems to come much more easily. I feel
as if I were on firm ground. I put together the things that have already
turned out well. I drape my fabrics according to established principles. But plenty of things always happen to force me to change what
seemed just right. It reminds me of Penelope's labor.[37]

What happens during the first fittings?

Now we are in the midst of the drama. The first fitting is almost
always disappointing. The canvas is only an outline but an accurate
outline. As far as the final dress is concerned the fitting is what
the chrysalis is to the butterfly. Raw material and scissors take
charge. I have to win a battle with reality, carve a statue out of
a block of marble.[38]

Certain silhouettes are more challenging than others?

To bring to life a collection composed of 175 "looks" means coming
up with 175 dresses to be shown, plus the coats and jackets accompa-
nying them. Therefore there are about 220 models to be created.
And almost as many hats, not to mention gloves, shoes, jewels,
and handbags, which are specially designed.[39] As a general rule,
the models I believe are promising disconcert the public at first,
because the eye needs to get used to them. The very person who
has demanded novelty at any price becomes recalcitrant when
presented with it. I have been insulted routinely and frequently
over my career, for showing first long dresses, then short dresses,
then "pigeon breasts," then flat bosoms, then accentuated waistlines,
and then looser waistlines.[40]

Finally, the long-awaited moment arrives: the fashion show.

Last we decide on the order of the show. The last two days pass
in a strange kind of silence. The whole establishment puts its heart
into the work. I have no time to be nervous. This is the calm before
the storm. The workrooms are quiet. Apparently no one has anything
to do. From time to time a last-minute model makes its appearance.
Or an unsuccessful costume that I absolutely have to fix. I wish I could
run away. I wish that a sudden catastrophe, no matter how fatal, would
keep the collection from being shown. I wish I could die. On the
avenue people are beginning to gather near the door.[41]

And yet, seen from the outside, everything
seems planned with extreme precision.

The showing of a collection has this in common with the opening
of a play: the first exposure to specialists in order for them to weigh
in with their opinions is exceptionally important. I believe it is fair
to say that fashion writers generally know their business better than
theater critics. But this does not stop a couturier from brooding over
his collection with the terror of an author whose play is about to face
the floodlights of opening night. Twice a year I have to endure this
terrible torment. Some people find it adds excitement to the game.
Personally, I hate it much as I used to hate exams at school. My friends,
in an attempt to soothe my nerves, tell me that this appalling hurdle is
the best defense against growing old, and I pretend to believe them.[42]

How are seating arrangements determined?

As the great day draws near, the nerve center of the building shifts
from the studio to the salon. The publicity department becomes the
heart that beats out impatience into the general bloodstream. Homeric
problems of hierarchy arise: 300 people need to be squeezed into
two rooms and an entresol when, along with the narrow hallway
for the models, there is space for 250 at most. A justly inflexible and
complicated protocol determines the precedence of one guest over
another; and it is in fact our dearest and most intimate friends who
find themselves relegated to the doorways, corners, and staircases.[43]

The exact placement of each seat is a study in itself.
There are habitués, who will be mortally offended by any change;
writers who have switched from one paper to another; friends who
have fallen out from one season to the next; publications that have
either sprung into existence or grown in importance since the last
collection. Each journalist must have a place that adequately reflects
both the importance of the paper for which he writes and his
personal prestige. Even so, the seating plan sometimes has to be
modified because of unforeseen circumstances.[44]

The order for showing the models must also be closely studied.

The order of the show obeys certain fixed laws of precedence:
first come the suits, then the day dresses, then more formal ensembles,
the cocktail dresses, the short evening dresses, finally the long evening
dresses and the ball gowns, which are generally spectacularly embroidered. A wedding dress ends the show. But the classic order needs
a certain dramatic quality, as well as exceptional models. . . As for
the shock troops, those startling designs that are the symbols of
new lines, they are placed toward the middle of the show. It is these
"Trafalgars" that make the covers or important pages of magazines;
these are the models that determine the fashion of today and also of
tomorrow. About an hour into the show, they recapture the audience's
wandering attention.[45]

What can you tell us about the atmosphere backstage?

Imagine a dressing room made to hold twelve mannequins, and in
which there are thirty people all told: the *premières*, the *secondes*,
twelve or fourteen mannequins, two hairdressers in action, the people
in charge of accessories, plus 200 dresses, gloves, hats, muffs, parasols,
necklaces, shoes . . . There are indescribable scenes reminiscent of a
Marx Brothers film.[46] I admit my anxiety, although I try to master
and above all to hide it, when the parade is running a bit late —
and in silence. It's no use telling myself that silence means attention.
I prefer applause!

Applause restores my hope. At these moments I forget
the commercial future of the collection. I live only for these first few
hours, this first contact, this first success. The rest is of little importance. The child is born; to know whether it is beautiful and to guess
at its future one has to wait until tomorrow.[47]

How do the models deal with the pressure?

A mannequin must in fact show nothing of the fever of the dressing
room. She must act as if she had had the time to prepare her beauty at
leisure, and as if the greatest calm and serenity reigned in her heart and
mind.[48] They are unbearable and charming. That is why you love them.
What would this fashion business be, composed of life and movement as
it is, if all these dresses had to be hung on wooden figures? I dare not think
of it! As for me, on the day of the first show the dressing room is a picture
of hell, whereas to the public it has to appear as a bouquet — and I hope
that it really will be a bouquet of gay flowers and not a wreath![49]

Once the show is over, how do you feel?

For me, the terrible moment has arrived when I have to face the voices,
laughter, cheers, and sighs, when up until now I have heard only the
echoes of them behind my gray satin curtains. I abandon my vantage
point and relinquish my temporary deafness to surrender myself to the
warmth and affection of my friends. I call it a terrible moment, because
it is now that I reach the climax of the terror I have been experiencing ever
since the beginning of the show. But it is also a delicious moment, because
I now see for the first time the beloved faces of my friends, whose presence
I previously only suspected. While the Champagne goes around, I shake
outstretched hands, kiss scented cheeks, receive the congratulations of
my staff, and listen to the delightfully exaggerated words of praise that are
being applied to my collection: divine, adorable, ravishing. My first name
is on everyone's lips; I want to thank every single person in the room and
tell him or her how happy I am to have provided satisfaction. Intoxicated
with noise and joy, I scarcely have time to reply to the journalist who asks
me which dress is my favorite: They are all my favorites, I answer. They are
my children, and I love them all equally well.[50]

*If you hadn't been a fashion designer,
what would you have liked to do?*

I wanted to be an architect; as a dressmaker I have to follow the laws
and principles of architecture. One of the things you mentioned earlier
and that I have in abundance is fabric. And fabric leads me directly to
architecture. It is far from absurd to speak of the architecture of a dress.
One builds a dress according to the direction of the fabric — that is
the secret of couture and it is a secret that is dependent on the first rule
of architecture: obeying gravity. The way fabric falls — and the line
and balance of a dress springs from this — depends on its direction;
this will differ depending on whether there is, in the words of the
profession, a "straight cut" or a "bias cut." These are the two principal
cuts, with the straight being more traditional, and the bias more
ornate. One's approach to the arrangement of different fabrics, and
one's ability to segue seamlessly from one to the other: these are the
principal secrets of our profession. First and foremost, the cut allows us
to stylize certain shapes of the body. It might be banal to say so, but one
cannot overestimate the importance of the cut. The cut is inescapably
linked to the sleek, pared down look of today's dresses, free of the frills
of yesteryear, and whose apparent simplicity hearkens back to outfits
from antiquity.[51]

In other words, you build your silhouettes architecturally.

In today's fashion the most carefully shaped part of a dress is the
armature — though that word is not really appropriate. Basically, we're
talking about the muslin models the seamstresses use to make adjust-
ments. The *toile* retains the memory of forms thanks to the iron, which
truly sculpts the material.[52] My dresses always reflect everyday life, with
its emotions, its outpourings of tenderness and joy.[53]

Does your preoccupation with the female form express
itself through your so-called "endless variations"?

Yes, an unending variation on the same theme: the female body,
a single note upon which a couturier should compose a thousand
variations, much like the musician who only has the seven notes of
a scale to work with.[54] The art of the dressmaker is to find the right
lines to exalt the female form.[55]

You have always championed the use of accessories.
How do you feel about their influence?

Accessories are of utmost importance. Ugly gloves, bad shoes, cheap hats, all of these things can spoil a dress or a suit. Accessories are a very important facet of elegance. In the United States a good black sweater and a simple pleated skirt can form a basic wardrobe if matched with the right accessories. Color and style must be respected. They set the tone of the whole look; they are the key aspect of it. Personally I would prefer to see a badly dressed woman wearing neutral colors rather than an aggressively dressed woman with colors and accessories that have been chosen without a discriminating eye. In my opinion American women are not always successful in this regard because they buy enormous amounts of things. Their clothes are often overloaded, though I am aware that they have to take into account the climate, not to mention lifestyle and light.[56]

Do you have an archetype in mind of the ideal
woman for whom you design your clothes?

No, I am not thinking of only one woman. As I said earlier, I always imagine the average woman: not too dark, not too pale, and I am often surprised to hear people say that my dresses are made for small women. Don't forget that for me, size is not an essential ingredient to elegance.[57] Nothing makes me happier than seeing a fashion become hugely popular. That is my constant aim. Of course I do know that my work is geared to a certain class of women, the elegant class. But fashion is for women the world over — for women in general. I would like nothing more than to make every woman look and feel like a duchess. Those on the lowest rungs of the social ladder should be striving to move upward, this is a natural law. But I always find very charming a pretty farm girl who looks like a pretty farm girl, or a charming duchess who looks like a charming duchess. What I don't like to see is a duchess who looks like a farmer's wife.[58]

You undoubtedly want me to talk about the women who end up wearing my dresses: that is to say, my 800 clients. . . I have said this before: my ambition has always been to be considered a decent craftsman, and at the same time, a good purveyor. For a dressmaker as well as for a businessman, satisfying the clients is the most important duty of all.

When the clients come, the salon takes on another aspect. It is always packed (we have 25,000 visitors each season), and stops being a place where work is done, to become a spot where one has fun — at least the clients do. It's like the last salon where conversations occur. My clients are all talkative. What do they chat about? The holidays, the latest successful play, the latest Parisian scandal, and, first and foremost, the collections of my rivals. So what kind of talk does one hear chez Dior? Things like this: "Oh, sweetheart, Balenciaga is sensational." "Givenchy is touched with genius." "Balmain's wedding dress is sublime . . ." "Chanel is simply divine!"[59]

Still, your designs are destined for a luxury clientele.

The dresses that we make are, I admit, accessible only to the happy few. I don't consider this a problem. Every society needs an elite. There are in my opinion at least two important justifications for couture. First of all, it is a prototype, and therefore costly. Also, it represents a treasure trove of conscientious craftsmanship and triumphant, even masterful handiwork — hundreds of hours of labor. That is its intrinsic value. It also has another, inestimable importance. It is comparable to the first raspberry, or first lily of the valley. It is ahead of its time, and therefore completely unique. Depending on how it is worn today, couture will determine what is fashionable in Paris, and in the rest of the world, tomorrow.[60]

How do you price your dresses?

The pink slips of paper that help me to set the prices of the clothes are beginning to pile up. It may surprise my readers to learn that I personally set the prices, when generally speaking I have nothing to do with the administrative or sales side of the business. But the price of a dress is of fundamental importance. Every model is the subject of a detailed file, stating the hours of work spent on it, the cost of the work done by hand, and the price of the material. By adding to this a percentage of the overhead, taxes, and the necessary profit, one gets a very good idea of the price at which a dress ought to be sold.[61]

How do French and American women differ,
sartorially speaking?

Let me begin with a few critical comments about how Frenchwomen dress. I hate, when I'm walking in the street, to see how sloppily attired they are: their hair, their wrinkled clothes, their unpolished shoes. As for American women, after two weeks in New York, I was overwhelmed by their excessive meticulousness. Super-sophistication is the main trap that American women need to avoid. I like individuality and unaffectedness. You need to find a balance between your fashion personality and reality — and that has to be your own character. The tastelessness of Frenchwomen hurts me terribly.

When I was in New York I suffered from the coldness, the sophistication of all that was over-polished. There should be some kind of middle ground. Women don't need to look like fashion plates, or like they just got back from their dressmaker. Personality should always trump fashion sense. When I design my models I am forced to act as a couturier, and exaggerate the line. However, I count on everyday life to humanize somewhat the rather drastic effects of my designs.[62]

Where do you find ideas and inspiration?

My inspiration is both unconscious and imperious. I sketch very rapidly, after having thought long and hard. I see a silhouette and mull it over in my mind. I can't really say where fashion comes from, but I can't work any other way. My newest collection springs from the preceding one, through eliminating some aspects and exaggerating others. In its own way, it is organic.[63]

What lessons can be learned from the history of couture?

It wasn't until Worth that the designer began signing his creations. And even then it was the empress's fashion, Second Empire fashion, and the reign of the crinoline lasted as long as that of Napoléon III. The "Worth era" was really the "Eugénie era." The nineteenth century put the designer in the spotlight. He was no longer known to only a few insiders, the way Rose Bertin was in Versailles, or Leroy at the Tuileries. His name was on everybody's lips; he was a character. And yet, he was not, literally speaking, a designer. In cinematic parlance, we would say that Paquin and Doucet were producers rather than directors. Their job was to choose among the *petites gravures*, the drawings proposed by freelance designers to each house.[64]

Ultimately, who creates fashion?

Actually it is the public which creates this spirit. It is made up of several elements. The first is the atmosphere of the moment — what is going on in the world; the second is logic; the third chance; and the fourth the choice made by the magazines. Among the large number of ideas which are put forward at every collection and at every season, only those which were successful and which, for that reason, will constitute the new fashions are remembered. How many times have we been disappointed to see passed over a model on which we were counting to make a hit! No doubt the reason is that it was not the right moment for it. These unnoticed ideas often reappear a season or two later. This time they are a hit — no one knows why. They are in tune with the mood of the day, and it is only then that they catch on. In a word, the dress designer proposes, woman disposes — often aided or guided by the magazines.[65]

What are the distinctive features of a fashion house?

A couture house is like an invalid. Every day you have to take its temperature, feel its pulse, find its blood pressure, and order analyses made. You have to behave like a doctor who is taking no chances.

That's why the business condition of the house is plotted on a graph paper, like a temperature chart, and hangs on the wall in the manager's office. With this chart he can tell at a glance whether his business is healthy.[66]

Do you consider fashion a safe bet, or something
that fluctuates, like the stock market?

One thing is certain: fashion is always a reaction to what was previously fashionable. Secondly: fashion successively, and alternately, exaggerates certain forms, and in that way displaces and renews our attention — our attraction, too. It is curious to see how, from generation to generation, what we find charming changes, while certain aspects remain consistent; and these aspects are in turn influenced by external circumstances such as war and peace, alliances, production patterns, trade, discoveries, as well as by the thoughts and work of this or that powerful writer or artist.[67]

How do you get a handle on the Zeitgeist?

I think that each designer, through his own methods and approach, manages more or less to put his finger on general trends. A novelist or a playwright creates a form out of ideas that are supposedly "floating around." In fashion, we're not necessarily dealing with ideas, but with proportions. Each year, for each season, the female sartorial style has a correct proportion — and it will be out of fashion the following season. Why? Because through the process of imitation that essentially characterizes fashion, these proportions will become banal. Boredom is what makes a certain fashion outdated, creating a perpetual need for renewal.[68]

Are you saying fashion cannot be made to last?

To quote Cocteau, "Fashion dies young." It is therefore normal that it should move through life at a faster pace than history.[69]

What is it about the fashion business that moves you?

A fashion devoid of a certain poetic resonance is worthless. All the fashions I have created have come from the heart. When a woman tells me: I feel different when I am wearing one of your dresses, she is giving me the highest compliment I could imagine.[70]

Why do people say that fashion is useless?

Fashion is not any more or less useful than poetry or popular music. With the passing of the centuries, fashion acquires a kind of dignity; it becomes a witness to its time. Ours is the era of the image. When we remember time past, we immediately see a certain way of dressing. Therefore, in this century, which has been attempting to destroy all of its most terrifying secrets one after the other, what could be a more noble occupation than attempting to create a lovely new secret, every six months or so? Couldn't one on the contrary see that as a kind of wisdom?[71]

Could you please say a few words about elegance?

A problem that I often come across is the problem of deciding the difference between what is elegant and what is "dressed up." What is dressed up is not necessarily chic. What is elegant is not always the right choice. That which is provocative can be chic, but it is not always the correct choice.[72]

Yves Saint Laurent has worked with you.

He is my spiritual heir.[73]

You have experienced global success.
How would you describe it?

Success is nothing other than work, work, and more work.[74]

What does couture represent for you?

Couture is first and foremost the marriage of form and fabric.[75]

And lastly, what is the goal of couture?
What is its raison d'être?

The supreme goal of couture is to embellish rather
than dress, to adorn rather than to clothe.[76]

—◦ NOTES ◦—

1   "La Mode a perdu son Roi," *Paris Match*,
    November 1, 1957, 4.

2   Christian Dior, *Christian Dior
    and I*, trans. Antonia Fraser
    (New York: Dutton, 1957), 10.

3   Dior, *Christian Dior and I*, 11.

4   Christian Dior, conversation with
    Alice Perkins and Lucie Noël,
    January 10, 1955, transcript, Centre de
    Documentation Mode, Musée des Arts
    Décoratifs, Paris.

5   Christian Dior, "Dior par Dior,
    les carnets secrets d'un grand couturier,"
    Le Temps de Paris, May 16, 1956, 12.

6   Christian Dior, *Talking About Fashion*,
    trans. Eugenia Sheppard (New York:
    Putnam, 1954), 6.

7   Dior, *Talking About Fashion*, 7–8.

8   Dior, *Talking About Fashion*, 13.

9   Dior, *Talking About Fashion*, 15.

10 Dior, *Talking About Fashion*, 16–17.

11 Dior, *Talking About Fashion,* 18–19.

12 Dior, *Talking About Fashion,* 26–27.

13 Dior, *Talking About Fashion,* 25–26.

14 Dior, *Talking About Fashion,* 8.

15 Dior, *Talking About Fashion,* 20–21.

16 Dior, *Talking About Fashion,* 8–9.

17 Dior, *Talking About Fashion,* 21.

18 Dior, *Talking About Fashion,* 19.

19 Christian Dior, "Les révolutions dans la couture, comment on fait la mode," *Le Figaro Littéraire,* June 8, 1957.

20 Dior, *Christian Dior and I,* 31.

21 Dior, "Dior par Dior, les carnets secrets d'un grand couturier," May 16, 1956, 12.

22 Dior, *Talking About Fashion,* 28–29.

23 Dior, "Dior par Dior," May 16, 1956, 12.

24 Dior, "Dior par Dior," May 16, 1956, 12.

25 Dior, "Dior par Dior," May 16, 1956, 12.

26 Dior, "Dior par Dior," May 16, 1956, 12.

27 Dior, "Dior par Dior," May 16, 1956, 12.

28 Dior, "Dior par Dior," May 16, 1956, 12.

29 Dior, *Christian Dior and I,* 35–36.

30 Dior, *Talking About Fashion,* 29–30.

31 Dior, *Christian Dior and I,* 45.

32 "Christian Dior, Dictateur de la Mode," *Sélection du Reader's Digest,* June 1957, 45.

33 Dior, "Les révolutions dans la couture, comment on fait la mode."

34 Dior, *Talking About Fashion,* 34.

35 Dior, *Talking About Fashion,* 35–36.

36 *Samedi Soir,* February 11, 1950

37 Dior, *Talking About Fashion,* 66–67.

38 Dior, *Talking About Fashion,* 65.

39 Dior, *Talking About Fashion,* 51.

40 Dior, "Dior par Dior," May 12, 1956, 15.

41 Dior, *Talking About Fashion,* 73–74.

42 Dior, "Dior par Dior," May 8, 1956, 15.

43 Dior, "Dior par Dior," May 8, 1956, 15.

44 Dior, "Dior par Dior," May 8, 1956, 15–16.

45 Dior, "Dior par Dior," May 8, 1956, 15.

46 Dior, *Talking About Fashion,* 80–81.

47 Dior, *Talking About Fashion,* 82.

48 Dior, *Talking About Fashion,* 82.

49 Dior, *Talking About Fashion,* 79–80.

50 "La Mode a perdu son Roi," 7.

51 Christian Dior, *Conférences écrites par Christian Dior pour la Sorbonne, 1955–1957* (Paris: Editions du Regard/Institut Français de la Mode, 2003), 43–44.

52 Dior, *Conférences écrites par Christian Dior pour la Sorbonne, 1955–1957,* 44–45.

53 "La Mode a perdu son Roi," 4.

54 Dior, *Conférences écrites par Christian Dior pour la Sorbonne, 1955–1957,* 49.

55 "La Mode a perdu son Roi," 4.

56 Christian Dior, conversation with Alice Perkins and Lucie Noël, January 10, 1955.

57 Christian Dior, conversation with Alice Perkins and Lucie Noël, January 10, 1955.

58 Christian Dior, conversation with Alice Perkins and Lucie Noël, January 10, 1955.

59   "Dior par Dior," May 13–14, 1956, 23.

60   Dior, "Les révolutions dans la couture, comment on fait la mode."

61   Dior, "Dior par Dior," May 8, 1956, 16.

62   Christian Dior, conversation with Alice Perkins and Lucie Noël, January 10, 1955.

63   Christian Dior, conversation with Alice Perkins and Lucie Noël, January 10, 1955.

64   Dior, "Les révolutions dans la couture, comment on fait la mode."

65   Dior, *Talking About Fashion,* 38–39.

66   Dior, *Talking About Fashion,* 104–05.

67   Dior, *Conférences écrites par Christian Dior pour la Sorbonne,* 47–48.

68   Dior, *Conférences écrites par Christian Dior pour la Sorbonne,* 46–47.

69   "La Mode a perdu son Roi," 4.

70   "Christian Dior, Poète de la Mode," *Samedi Soir,* February 11, 1950.

71   Dior, "Les révolutions dans la couture, comment on fait la mode."

72   Christian Dior, conversation with Alice Perkins and Lucie Noël, January 10, 1955.

73   Jack Garofalo and Michel Simon, "Dior," *Paris Match,* November 9, 1957, 72.

74   "Christian Dior, Poète de la Mode," *Samedi Soir,* February 11, 1950.

75   "La Mode a perdu son Roi," 4.

76   *L'Aurore,* August 1953.

MADAME GRÈS

*Madame Grès, you have been working in haute couture
for more than five decades, have you not?*

The words *haute couture* always surprise me: What do you mean
by *couture*? I am just a good seamstress. For me, haute couture means
being a good artisan. You see, good work comes from the imagination. All manual labor stimulates the mind.[1]

Why did you choose fashion to express your talents?

I like to accentuate the beauty, personality, and individual movements
of women I dress. A couture dress is a second skin. Each woman has
her own unique comportment and figure. . . I see my clients transformed during a fitting. It is a miracle to see this.[2] I try to bring out
the best in them. I try always to give them something new.[3]

How do you begin designing?

I prepare my muslin, I pin it . . . then I cut, I sculpt the cloth . . . But you know, this is simply what any good seamstress does! I start working a month and a half before the first show, but then I work day and night until the last possible moment: I cannot work in any other way . . . it's probably stage fright . . . On the other hand, when I have hit my stride nothing can stop me! I train my seamstresses myself: they share a devotion for good work, and they also deserve admiration . . . You asked me how I got into this business . . . I loved couture, and I wanted to adorn bodies . . . A woman's body is so beautiful, so precious. It is not a piece of furniture; it lives, and breathes, it moves, and finding what looks good on it can take some time. Fashion exists to beautify women; that is why the profession of those who dress them is so noble.[4]

Some say that Parisian couture has lost its aura.

No, I don't believe it! There are still many of us who are maintaining the tradition. On the contrary, we are staunchly defending this industry because we don't want it to disappear! It needs to stay alive, and perpetuate itself. We are the only ones who consistently use the most beautiful material, thus providing a livelihood to so many marvelous craftsmen! Because we find it important to work with beautiful fabrics, those that stimulate the imagination. Haute couture is and will forever remain a melting pot of ideas and experimentation![5] Couture is a true ideal. I have been asked about the problems of couture, but at the House of Grès we have no difficulties. The workers are happy. People gladly give extra time for collections. Yes, there are less craftsmen than in years past, but we have in Paris the finest handwork available. It does exist. Quality is enduring.[6]

And yet, you seem to be critical as well.

Oh, I'm just feeling cranky . . . It won't last. All of my ideas will soon again be inspired by all that is noble, and not only the fabrics . . . The whole world has decided to produce couture, and embark in this profession without taking the time to learn it. The absurd things one sees . . .

Well, this is just a stage, we are returning to beauty, to beautiful ideas, to the *costume* and not the disguise! We need to preserve ourselves . . . There should be no leaks whatsoever before a collection; it should be a true surprise . . . We need to protect our profession: that is what I have always done![7] People say there is a new energy in the couture these days, but I really don't know. I feel the energy has always been there. Young people today are interested in and appreciate quality. I see it in my young clients. People realize that couture is truth — couture is inspirational. The couture goes beyond the frontiers of the house that it is designed in. The couture influences everything. The couture is my life.[8] Let me give you an example of the power of the couture. I was in Russia in 1969 — or was it in 1968? — for a three-day tour with my couture collection. One day I showed to the government officials, but the other two days I showed to the people — in large public auditoriums. The people came from far away — they were poor but they paid a few rubles or somesuch to see the show. I have never seen a reaction like this. They could not imagine that clothes such as I showed even existed. They couldn't get over it. They cried. It was a very emotional event for me. One that I will never forget.[9]

That said, how important is ready-to-wear?

The importance of prêt-à-porter? Ooh la la. The couture always gives the ideas to prêt-à-porter. The prêt-à-porter designers are always influenced by the couturiers. I feel that prêt-à-porter has indeed given the woman in the street a better, neater appearance, but couture is the creative key. It is a grand work — it is truth — couture brings something into the world.[10] The couture and the pret are two completely different genres of creation. Both are interesting. The ready-to-wear can bring the woman things she can't buy in couture and they aren't copies of couture.[11]

Is it a question of means?

Well, one can go to a Uniprix and choose inexpensive clothes that go well together and that embellish the body rather than make it unattractive. Every woman has something beautiful in her. It is up to her to discover and take advantage of it. It is not a question of money.[12]

What advice do you have for today's modern woman?

Do not try to grab attention. All these young women with enormous earrings and sloppy hair only want to be noticed, out of sheer vanity. Since the war, working women have abandoned their children far too much. That is why we are seeing this kind of behavior. But things will soon get back to normal.[13] It's a shame that hats disappeared. They looked so good, you could change them depending on the dress — and the materials were always very beautiful.[14]

Tell us about the profession of couturier.

One must have courage to be a couturier. Unhappily, a maison of couture is a business. It is very, very difficult. Each season, a couture collection is judged on the strength of the designs you present. It is like you are nude for the whole world to see.[15]

How did you start out?

In 1934 I wanted to be a sculptor, but my parents were against it.
I had a friend who was the *première* of a big house, and in three months
she taught me to cut cloth. I began alone with a sewing machine in
a tiny room in the Eighth Arrondissement. I created a collection of
models that were immediately successful. The following year, using
the name Alix, I became an associate of a couture house situated at the
Faubourg Saint-Honoré. I designed four collections a year. Then came
the war, and the exodus . . . When I returned to Paris I had to start all
over again. Without a backer, I set up shop on rue de la Paix.[16]

Where did the name Alix come from?

It was my nickname.[17]

Do you still have a sculptor's approach?

I feel like what I'm doing is living sculpture: I begin by modeling
on the body, I work on the curves, the fall of the fabric, the balance
of the forms. The thing that attracted me to couture was the desire
to find the golden ratio, to celebrate the human body.[18] The clothes
logically followed the sculpture; the working of material doesn't
change. You also have the support of the body in making couture
and in sculpture.[19] I work with my hands, with a mass of fabric,
like a sculptor with clay.[20]

How important is fabric in your creative process?

When you know the sense of a fabric, you know everything.[21]
Let it live, that fabric. It will take the path it must take.[22]

Do you have a favorite color?

For color I like white. White for me is peace — order and peace . . .[23]

Is the past a source of inspiration?

We never look back; we're always in the future.[24] The past does not
interest me in the least; I am obsessed with the future. I don't like the
old, and I forget my collections once they are done.

Obviously, there were very beautiful things before, but life has moved on, obligations have evolved, and so clothing changes, too. For example, one sees more and more women who don't have the time to go home to change at night, so we have to create clothes that are suitable from morning to night. Fashion evolves; so does life. But one must keep a sense of form, and one must love the beauty of a woman's body.[25]

You are known for the draped jersey dress
— it seems to have become your specialty.

My specialty? No, I know how to do other things, too.[26] I first imagine my dresses in my head, then let the proportions of the body guide me . . . to resculpt their form.[27] From the beginning I didn't want to do what others were doing in any way; and I wasn't able to because I didn't have the knowledge. That was one reason I took the material and worked directly on it. I used the knowledge I had, which was sculpture.[28]

How do you manage to make your lines so distinct?

Because each woman has a different personality . . .
I mean, we're not stereotyped, are we?[29]

How do you define elegance?

Elegance, for me, is a permanent state of grace.[30]

How does one attain it?

The elegant woman is discreet usually; she dresses simply and *comme il faut*; she knows how to use her imagination without being eccentric: she is both sophisticated and sober, and she knows how to choose that one outfit that looks good in every circumstance. The one that makes her feel at home everywhere.[31] Everything depends on whether or not you have been taught to make the right choices.

Simplicity and elegance are never boring: you can never get enough of them, and one single detail manages to suggest that touch of gaiety that only you have! . . . Oh, the hemline? Halfway down the calf. That is the most elegant; all legs look good in it. However, if around fifty or sixty a woman's figure becomes a little stouter, it should be shortened . . . two or three inches above the knee, it makes you look younger, it has a jauntiness to it![32]

And what is the difference between being elegant and being chic?

If a woman is chic, it is in her nature. She can be elegant but lacking something if she doesn't have that *je ne sais quoi* . . . She can be pretty, ravishing, delicious, but if that spark, that gesture is missing . . . It's all a question of personality.[33]

What do you consider to be a sign of the most egregious bad taste?

You shouldn't undress a woman; you have to respect her. Nudity is indecent. Sweaters shouldn't be too tight, and you need well-styled hair. Incidentally, cavemen had too much hair; you can't keep everything. However outright shaving of the head might be too radical a course of action . . .[34]

There is a real tendency toward androgyny in fashion these days. What do you think of the blurring of lines between genders?

Ah, but our bodies are not at all the same! Let us be truly proud of our differences! If we erase all signs of femininity how can we expect men to recognize, appreciate, and respect us? I am certain that you have already noticed that your movements, your appearance are not the same depending on whether you are wearing a dress or a pair of pants . . . and unconsciously, the attitude of the men around you is also different: believe me, clothing has a very great influence on individual behavior. Try to remember this in order to live in greater harmony, and better enjoy your freedom.[35]

What role did the Americans play in your success?

They gave me courage. They were so enthusiastic. I was very surprised; I was crying when I saw that enthusiasm.[36] What I like about the Americans is that they know right away what's new without having it shouted at them.[37]

How would you describe your clientele?

My clients are very special, special women. I admit that sometimes they do inspire my work. Most of the women are French, but we have many from America, Brazil, and Greece. The Americans are wonderful to work with. American women seem to like different ideas, different shapes. They have an appreciation for sculpture. They are modern and they appreciate simplicity. And on top of that, American women have such good rib cages and backs. And such long legs.[38]

Do you look at the work of your competitors?

The others? I am not interested in what anybody else does. I have never in my career attended a showing of another designer. You must always find your ideas in yourself — not the direction of others. I do not believe in studying what other couturiers do. The couture is an individualistic manner of cut and working with fabric. It has nothing to do with outside influences. It is not worth the pain to work if you do not do something unique and coming from you alone. I have even refused designers who wanted to come and see my collections. The couture should be individual.[39] When you are alone, you are different and your mind works. I do everything myself. I don't follow any of the other couturiers. Everyone should bring to their work some part of themselves.[40]

Do you have any recurring inspirations?

I work too much, and have no time for outside influences. In fact, I really don't admire such-and-such a school or type of creation. You have to judge each thing individually. You can't open your mind if you feel you have to stay in a certain style or follow a certain school.[41] But, you might go on a beautiful trip, and take a few things from what you see, and create a unique piece of work, a uniquely French piece of work. This is what the great couturier knows how to do . . . [42]

What about street fashion?

I never go down into the street. I don't have time to sit at the terrasse of a café and people-watch. I spend most of my time in my apartment and the atelier, preparing our collections.[43] I didn't go down to the street. I moved up to it.[44]

How do you see your era?

You can't stop the evolution of things. You can't say whether they're bad or good. Each day, there's an evolution. I don't like to compare the present with the past.[45]

Is there an important trait to have as a designer?

Ignorance is a very important thing — it has purity and innocence. It leads you to try things that others wouldn't dare attempt.[46]

Would it be fair to say that you have dedicated your life to couture?

I don't have what is known as a private life. My life is entirely given over to the house and to the people who work in it. I think that, when all is said and done, creating is for me the only way to exist . . . The days fly by, identical to one another. And my family has certainly suffered much more than I have. I tore myself away from my family, from a loving home, from the intimacy of family gatherings and parties and vacations. And it is not only my own family that was neglected; I was obligated to sacrifice the private lives of all those who work with me.[47] Freedom comes from within.[48]

Any regrets?

I had to choose: life or work. I have a daughter I adore. I had a marvelous husband. My father, my mother. I sacrificed them all. Any regrets? If I do have any, I'll keep them to myself.[49]

⟞ NOTES ⟝

1   F. Vergnaud, "Rencontre avec Madame Grès," *Marie France*, October 1976, 49.

2   Marian McEvoy, "Gres Matter," *Women's Wear Daily*, February 15, 1977, 6.

3   "Something New — Key to Alix Grès' Success," *Women's Wear Daily*, October 27, 1969, 14.

4   Vergnaud, "Rencontre avec Madame Grès," 49.

5   Vergnaud, "Rencontre avec Madame Grès," 49.

6   McEvoy, "Gres Matter," 7.

7   Vergnaud, "Rencontre avec Madame Grès," 49.

8   McEvoy, "Gres Matter," 6.

9   McEvoy, "Gres Matter," 6–7.

10   McEvoy, "Gres Matter," 6.

11   Ben Brantley, "Mme. Grès: An Original," *Women's Wear Daily*, November 1979, 34.

12   Chantal Zerbib, "'La femme n'est pas un clown' ou la mode vue par Madame Grès," *Lire*, May 1984, 85.

13   Zerbib, "'La femme n'est pas un clown,'" 84–85.

14   Zerbib, "'La femme n'est pas un clown,'" 85.

15   McEvoy, "Gres Matter," 6.

16   Indalecio Alvarez, "Madame Grès: Le grand mystère," *Paris Match*, December 1994, 56.

17   Edmonde Charles-Roux, "Madame Grès," *Vogue* (US) September 15, 1964, 98.

18   Fabienne Dagouat, "Madame Grès, tout simplement," *Le Matin*, July 28–29, 1984, 24.

19   Brantley, "Mme. Grès: An Original," 34.

20   Ingrid Bleichroeder, "Madame Gres," *Vogue* (UK), March 1984, 256.

21   François-Marie Banier, "Haute Couture 74/75: Portrait de Madame Grès," *Vogue* (France), September 1974, 171.

22   Banier, "Haute Couture 74/75: Portrait de Madame Grès," 172.

23   Bleichroeder, "Madame Grès," 256.

24   Brantley, "Mme. Grès: An Original," 34.

25   Zerbib, "'La femme n'est pas un clown' ou la mode vue par Madame Grès," 85.

26   Janie Samet, "La Vie au Féminin," *Le Figaro*, July 30, 1986, 17.

27   Alvarez, "Madame Gres: Le grand mystère," 54.

28   Brantley, "Mme. Grès: An Original," 34.

29   Vergnaud, "Rencontre avec Madame Grès," 49.

30   Alvarez, "Madame Gres: Le grand mystère," 54.

31   Dagouat, "Madame Grès, tout simplement," 24.

32   Vergnaud, "Rencontre avec Madame Grès," 49.

33   Bleichroeder, "Madame Grès," 256.

34   Zerbib, "'La femme n'est pas un clown' ou la mode vue par Madame Grès," 85.

35 Vergnaud, "Rencontre avec
    Madame Grès," *Marie France*, 49.

36 Brantley, "Mme. Grès: An Original," 34.

37 "Something New —
    Key to Alix Grès' Success,"14.

38 McEvoy, "Gres Matter," 7.

39 McEvoy, "Gres Matter," 7.

40 Sandra L. Rauffer, "Madame Grès's Story,"
    Revelations, November 20, 1978.

41 Brantley, "Mme. Grès: An Original," 34.

42 Vergnaud, "Rencontre avec
    Madame Grès," 49.

43 Zerbib, "'La femme n'est pas un clown'
    ou la mode vue par Madame Grès," 84.

44 Grès boutique. Print advertisement,
    Vogue (France), August 1980.

45 Brantley, "Mme. Grès: An Original," 34.

46 Bleichroeder, "Madame Gres," 256.

47 Sahoko Hata, *L'Art de Madame Grès*
    (Tokyo: Bunka Publishing Bureau, 1980),
    254.

48 Vergnaud, "Rencontre avec
    Madame Grès," 49.

49 Elisabeth Sancey, "La mode au temps
    de Madame Grès," *Paris Match*,
    March 24, 2011, 37.

PIERRE BALMAIN

Pierre Balmain, how did you get involved in fashion?

There are many ways into the world of haute couture. Some, like Lucien Lelong, inherited their business. Christian Dior, whose studies were cut short by family financial troubles, started work in an art gallery before he began selling designs to couturiers and modistes. For myself I do not remember a time when I was not interested in dress design and the intriguing play of materials against the feminine form. The world of fashion has always fascinated me, although I come from a background in which there were few couturiers and no one to encourage me in my vision.[1]

Tell us about the launch of your career.

My career began in the shadow of royalty, since it was the very week
of the wedding of Princess Marina and the Duke of Kent, in London,
that I began working for Molyneux, who had created her wardrobe.[2]
I can still see the young eighteen-year-old boy that I was, a little pale,
very long hair, in a suit made by the finest tailor in Chambéry. I was
studying at the Beaux-Arts when, driven by the need to make some
money, I went to show my sketches to Molyneux. He hired me, and
I began spending afternoons working for him on rue Royale, while
in the mornings I pursued my architecture studies. A short time later
he recommended that I work full-time in couture, and here I am.
For years, when I was a high school student or at the École des Beaux-
Arts I drew countless feminine figures in the margins of my note-
books; now that my profession is inventing dresses, architecture
has become increasingly important to me, and it is not rare to find
garden designs in the margins of the paper I use to sketch clothing.
This apparent paradox is not as remarkable as it may seem: I often
react and think as an architect might react and think.[3]

Let's return to your unexpected early success.

I took my first timid steps into the world of couture by selling
three fashion sketches to Robert Piguet for ninety francs.[4] I had
prepared the sketches as specimens in the hope of persuading
a couture house to offer me a job. I had never thought of anyone
buying them, but this was the next best thing, and although modest,
the payment thrilled me.[5]

*Do you have fond memories of your initial
encounter with Monsieur Piguet?*

Piguet had just opened a magnificent new salon with thick black
carpets, dark brown satin chairs, and mirrored walls, at 5 rue du
Cirque. His collection was being shown when I arrived. . . I was not
allowed to linger. Frightened perhaps that I might steal some ideas
if I watched the collection the receptionist hurried me straight
to Piguet's own studio.

It was a room in the attic with a red-tiled floor, and the
only furniture was a large cutting-table and some wooden stools.
I assumed this spartan contrast to the splendor of the salon was due
to the fact that Piguet had only recently opened his establishment.
He received me with a rather haughty politeness and rummaged
through my sketches in silence. Finally, still without comment,
he selected three, and rang for his secretary. Had I seen *The Barretts
of Wimpole Street*, then playing at the Théâtre des Ambassadeurs,
he asked, as she waited to escort me out; and he advised me to do
so before returning the following week to show him more sketches.
I was ushered down to the cashier, his cousin, whose immense girth
barely fitted into the tiny cubicle under the staircase. The secretary
muttered something and he gave me ninety francs.[6]

> *You had three letters of introduction: one for the
> Maison Lelong, one for Madame Lanvin, and one
> for Captain Molyneux.*

I tried Madame Lanvin first. I called several times and hung around
the waiting-room gazing hopefully at the office door impressively
inscribed with the single word, "Madame." Alas, without avail.
In the end the secretary told me politely: "Madame has no need
of you." So Madame never received me. Next, I went to see Lucien
Lelong at 16 avenue Matignon, where a heavy perfume hung in the air
and the whole house reeked of luxury. Monsieur Lelong received me
with courtesy and carefully studied my designs; "I would like
to help you," he said at last, "but really I have nothing for you at the
moment." He escorted me to the lift himself.[7]

> *And at long last you obtained an interview
> with Captain Molyneux.*

Grasping my letter of introduction I entered the graceful eighteenth
century building, 5 rue Royale. The commissionaire promptly sent
me to the back door, and I climbed a steep staircase to the office of the
studio secretary, an attractive girl in a pearl-gray dress and shoes to match.

She, too, had that mixture of exquisite politeness and haughty disdain which was becoming familiar to me as the typical couture air. She was horrified at the idea that I should expect to see Molyneux. "The captain is not receiving anyone at present," she said. "Leave your papers with me and come back . . ." I refused and insisted so emphatically . . . that finally, I was admitted. Captain Molyneux was standing in front of a blazing fire in a room with high windows, pearl-gray satin walls and mirrored covered pilasters. On the mirrored mantelpiece stood a rare Khmer head. He read through the letter and glanced through my drawings. Then, with an English accent, which amused me, he asked a few questions about my architectural studies. None of my drawings interested him but he would see me again the following week when he had more time.[8]

So you returned the following week.
What did he have to say to you then?

"Apart from the fact that we do not buy outside designs, I don't like these any better than the first ones," the Captain said, with a smile that softened his words. "All the same, I think we can do something with you. Carry on with your studies in the mornings, and work here in the afternoons. In a month's time I'll tell you whether to give up architecture or fashion-designing."[9]

You stayed with him for five years. What did you learn?

The first lesson I learned was that one should never try to add anything to a model but, rather, strip everything non-essential from its line. Like a writer, the couturier should say what he wants to say in as few words as possible. Any ornamental detail is valid only if it makes a constructive contribution to the dress.[10] He always believed in absolute simplicity that put duchesses into housemaid's dresses, and made them value the small white glazed collar more than their string of pearls.

I took away with me for always a taste of beige and a horror of gaudy details, and confidence that having begun my career in this excellent house, there were no limits to my hopes. That is what I owe to this elegant, aloof Englishman who held the fashion world in the palm of his hand, during the nineteen-thirties.[11]

In 1941 you went back to square one, chez Lelong.

I joined Lucien Lelong from Molyneux. He offered me a very remunerative contract and, the details settled, again courteously accompanied me to the lift.[12] I should have plenty to do, he told me, and what attracted me particularly was the fact that he was not keeping the pre-war designers ... Instead, he had taken on one young man who had worked for a short time with Robert Piguet, and whose name was then little known in the fashion world: Christian Dior. "You two will be entirely responsible for the collections," Lelong emphasized.[13]

Tell us about your first encounter with Christian Dior.

A rather fleshy man of average height entered. His hair was thinning, his eye sharp, nose long, and hand plump. "I am Christian Dior," he introduced himself. "I am delighted to meet you, Monsieur Balmain, but also terribly sorry to tell you that I can only work in silence. I do hope you will be kind enough to help me."[14]

How did you work together?

We had quite a different approach in our criticisms and suggestions. I am all of one piece, born under the sign of Taurus and utterly forth-right. ... Christian was gentleness and kindness itself. He preferred beating around the bush to the brutal assault. "A charming *robe*, my dear Pierre, but ..." And from that inoffensive "but" would cascade the most charmingly severe criticisms, all without any ulterior motive and with the sole aim of achieving a common success.[15]

Did you share the same workspace?

Christian took over a small room which had been a telephone booth, with padded walls that Lelong had had installed to prevent anyone overhearing private conversations . . . I camped, sketching and crumpling paper, amidst all the bustle of activity of the studio itself, where everyone came and went as though it were the Piccadilly Circus underground station.[16]

> *But truth be told, your mind was always set on opening your own house, right? That was a rather ambitious plan in 1945, just after the liberation of France.*

A miracle! I faced enormous difficulties. The war was barely over, and rationing was still in full force. We had to obtain from the Chambre Syndicale a quota of textile points and find a sympathetic ear among the manufacturers, to win their good graces for the allotment of a certain quantity of fabrics for this new house. Ironically, no sooner had I begun renting three floors of the building situated at 44 rue François-1er than it was requisitioned by the Ministry of Economic Affairs. To start a new house at that time seemed to be pure folly, especially since the international set had yet to return to Paris; nonetheless, the house opened on October 12, 1945.[17]

How did it all begin?

I founded a small company with almost no capital. I had sixteen seamstresses working on the only floor I was able to salvage from the requisition. In fact, the day we presented our very first collection, I had an argument with a military policeman who had come to throw me out. But I stood firm. We worked in every room of the second-floor apartment, even those that overlooked the courtyard, as well as in the kitchen, which had practically no light. Because of frequent electric current cuts, we used gas lamps. Thus it happened that one of the most luxurious models, in tulle entirely fashioned by hand in gathers and puffs, was destroyed by fire on the very day of delivery. The client needed that dress for an upcoming trip to the United States; she was upset and canceled her entire order: five dresses that we had already completed! It was a catastrophe, and almost put us out of business.[18]

Did you get any significant support from friends?

Gertrude Stein was good enough to write about my house the only article she ever published about fashion, and this had a very positive influence on the press in America and England, with *Time* publishing a photograph of one of my dresses as early as 1945. When I went to America in 1946, the triumphant reception I received from the Fashion Group was enough to go to the head of any novice. But, when all is said and done, my immediate success is no doubt attributable to the fact that I offered an image of feminine elegance that had not been seen since the pre-war years.[19]

You are originally from the Savoy region of France, are you not?

I was born at eight o'clock on Monday morning, May 18, 1914, at Saint-Jean-de-Maurienne, not far from Aix-les-Bains. My parents were well-to-do tradespeople.[20]

What was your first encounter with the world of couture?

I had met at St-Jean the daughter of Madame Premet, whose star shone brightly in the fashion world at the beginning of the century. She had come to the mountains for her health, and regaled me with stories of her mother's life: the glittering balls, the first nights, the glamour of the circles in which a successful couturier lived...

Although the interest had shown itself years before in dressing paper dolls with scraps of material, it was through Madame Premet, I think, that I definitely decided that I was going to be a famous Paris couturier, a creative fashion artist of worldwide reputation, directing business a that would give me entry to that elegant society world so far removed from my provincial origins as a tradesman's son in Savoy.[21]

Which fashion designers influenced you?

I studied as much as I could of this world of haute couture. I read eagerly reports of Paul Poiret's fabulous parties, the extravagances of Jean Patou at Biarritz, and detailed descriptions of Mademoiselle Chanel's château at Mesnil-Guillaume; but nothing fascinated me so much as the life of Monsieur Doucet, who was at the peak of his fame at the turn of the century. In his day, Monsieur Doucet dressed everyone who was anyone. His horses and carriages were celebrated, his house filled with treasures. He presented the city of Paris with his very valuable library, then, piqued by the fact that he was not awarded the *Légion d'Honneur* as quickly as he thought was his due, he refused to sign the necessary papers for a reconsideration of his case. Ironically, he saw to it that his secretary was invested with the order in recognition of his outstanding scholarship. Thereafter, if anyone asked Doucet whether he had the *Légion d'Honneur*, he replied with regal disdain: "Certainly — but it's my secretary who wears it."[22]

What are your strongest visual memories of your arrival in Paris?

I remember that first Sunday in 1932 when I arrived in Paris from my native Savoy. I came out of the metro and saw the place de la Concorde awash in floodlights. My throat tightened, my eyes filled with tears: the admirable harmony of the architecture of the city I dreamed of conquering moved me so. And I am sure my fellow couturiers have similar memories — since the vast majority of them also came to Paris from far-flung provincial towns. And what they now share with the world is their vision of the admirable facades of Gabriel, now known as the place de la Concorde, whose perfect symmetry seems almost accidental, so precisely mathematical is its composition. The evening dresses they design are fragile and constantly renewed interpretations of those fountains, as well as their message to the world — from this tiny portion of the universe called Paris, where an army of young women works for weeks to design the fantastic dresses that will enhance for a few hours the beauty of other women who lead lives and visit luxury spots that will forever remain a mystery to that first group.[23]

*What subject at university helped you most
in your creative approach?*

I am proud and happy to have trained to be an architect, no matter how brief was my time at the École Nationale Supérieure d'Architecture, for I deeply admire and respect that highly creative profession.

What I do is ephemeral by nature, since every few months that which was adored is destroyed. Thanks to a mysterious process, fashion is reborn each season, rising like a phoenix from its ashes. At heart couture's ideal is much more noble than mere appearance; it is a proportion, a form, the pursuit of an ideal: that of elegance.[24]

*Student of architecture, and then professional couturier:
what is the connection between these two activities?*

Both the architect and the couturier start with nothing and project their pure imagination upon materials. And yet that imagination is subservient to certain great fundamental principles of harmony, without which beauty of any kind is inconceivable. Also, both start with an idea and choose a way of expressing that idea — they impose a style and express themselves with their own personality, while also respecting an initial theme, for one the landscape, and for the other the female body. Just as an architect could never create a well-balanced work by deliberately ignoring the landscape, the couturier cannot invent something sound if he ignores the proportions of the body that he has been assigned. They are similar in their manner: the couturier handling his samples, the architect choosing his material — a certain kind of brick, or granite, or marble, or crystal that will quite exactly translate his thoughts. A couturier, in order to succeed, needs both the thick roughness of tweed and the evanescence of gauze or tulle.[25]

Yet there is one thing that makes the couturier's job more arduous: Couture is the architecture of movement. Nothing can be used by the couturier that hinders the expression of life. Architecture creates immobility, be it sumptuous or functional, practical or richly embellished. The couturier has to sew a tunic that can be all of those things, but that must also remain so no matter what position the woman wearing it adopts.

No architect has ever had to design a house that was expected to retain its balance and harmony in the event of an earthquake. I have seen dresses that were ruined by the slightest movement; and others that died when they remained immobile. One must have a profound knowledge of the human body and of how it moves.[26]

Any further thoughts you would care to share?

There is another, more fundamental difference between the architect and the couturier, and one that is quite profound: once the architect has traced his designs on paper, his project, the house or building, need only be transformed into being through material; whereas the couturier's sketch is nothing more than a spark that will give life to something that will escape him as soon as it is created, much like a child whose strong personality is often at odds with that of his parents.

A dress is constantly challenged until the day it is shown in public. It is much more malleable, because it is made out of a far less inflexible material; it changes form and its deeper meaning is also transformed. A dress imposes itself on its designer.[27]

You have designed clothes for the likes of Sophia Loren,
Ingrid Bergman, Martine Carol, Marlene Dietrich,
Brigitte Bardot, and Audrey Hepburn. What is the secret
to your popularity with such high-profile actresses?

What an embarrassing question. Maybe it is because my conception
of elegance — ease and simplicity — apparently meets the needs
of our time, though I also like to give my imagination free reign
when working with costumes. Perhaps, quite simply, because the
stars I see in Paris and in the course of my numerous trips sense
how much I enjoy finding solutions that allow their personalities
to appear in the most nuanced manner possible on the great master
of our contemporary world: the big screen.[28]

Could you share your thoughts on the cinema?

The camera is pitiless: it doesn't allow for a single error. Therefore,
the fittings must be perfect. That's stimulating for the couturier:
it keeps him on his toes. An image on the screen is a choice:
it fixes the character in his or her sartorial style at a given moment,
for the demanding eyes of the public. In her everyday life a woman
can fix a fault with a single movement of the hand. By definition,
cinema itself makes you change proportions and details — which
is challenging for a designer.[29]

Do you have any rules to live by?

Never make definitive statements. Once during an interview I told
a journalist — this was in the early years of my career — that a couturier
should let his work speak for itself. And since then I haven't stopped
... talking.[30]

In that case, here's another question for you:
Is ready-to-wear making haute couture unnecessary?

Absolutely not. A house such as ours cannot survive without haute couture. Which does not mean that haute couture hasn't changed. Whereas today we have a tendency to say that business is slow, our clientele is more important than ever. There will always be a demand for haute couture; for example, there are still in excess of one thousand clients at this very moment who wear haute couture, just as there is a specific clientele for jewelry, for designer furniture, or for rare objects.[31]

How do you feel about the American market?

Problems in America are linked to production — problems Americans resolve with admirable efficiency: a coat that comes out of a well-run factory goes through the hands of seventy-five people, flying from one pair to another in a sort of aerial chain. At each stage another ingredient is added before it comes out at the other end finished, ironed, ready to be sold, to be worn, to be thrown away . . . But America is not a country where you can launch fashions; as paradoxical as it may seem, by making bespoke dresses for a few elegant clients and without even intending to, Parisian couturiers invent the figure that will be emulated the following season by women all over the world.[32]

How would you define luxury?

Luxury is never ostentatious; it consists chiefly in refusing mediocrity.[33]

Are there ups and downs in a great designer's career?

A designer's skill bursts through quite suddenly and then maintains its standing — or not. In couture there are only downward spirals.[34]

How do you see yourself in the fashion family tree?

The oldest great designer alive today.[35] Unlike Schiaparelli, Courrèges, or Dior, who revolutionized fashion, I will remain the one who had the courage to refuse.[36]

What is the hardest thing to achieve?

Simplicity is the most difficult quality to give a dress. Jean Le Seyeux once said to me that in the music-hall nothing is more difficult to make than a costume for a nude: in couture nothing is more difficult to design than a simple dress.[37]

Do you have a code of conduct?

My guiding principle has always been that the dress is never a dress in and of itself; rather its value extends from the beautiful woman wearing it.[38] Throughout my career my dream has been to discover a line that involves no cutting at all — an aim complicated by the fact that I always try to remember that there is a female form inside the dress, and this must not be disguised. This — or at least keeping cutting to a minimum — may restrict the imagination, but only adds to the fascinating challenge of creation.[39]

Do you have a favorite feature of the female silhouette?

I like structured shoulders. So, to keep women from looking like wrestlers, I reinvented the raglan sleeve. The shoulders are structured but proportioned.[40]

Molyneux was the first to end each of his shows with a wedding dress. Do you have any similar rituals?

In an homage to the Duchess of Windsor, I always have a model marrying navy blue and black.[41]

What is your motto?

Rigor, always rigor.[42]

Is there anything you still dream about?

I have always dreamed of designing dresses.[43]

To conclude, you've been the subject of many articles in the press. What do you think your enduring public image will be?

"Designer to royalty" . . . That's the cliché fashion journalists tend to write when they want to attract readers.[44]

⸻ NOTES ⸻

1   Pierre Balmain, *My Years and Seasons* (London: Tassell, 1964), 2–3.

2   Press Kit for Pierre Balmain Spring Collection, 1976, Centre de Documentation Mode at the Musée des Arts Décoratifs.

3   Pierre Balmain, "Des rapports de l'Architecture avec la Couture." (Lecture presented to the Jeune Barreau, Brussels, Belgium, November 24, 1950), 3–4.

4   Press Kit for Pierre Balmain Spring Collection, 1976.

5   Balmain, *My Years and Seasons*, 31.

6   Balmain, *My Years and Seasons*, 30–31.

7   Balmain, *My Years and Seasons*, 32.

8   Balmain, *My Years and Seasons*, 33.

9   Balmain, *My Years and Seasons*, 34.

10   Balmain, *My Years and Seasons*, 36.

11   Balmain, *My Years and Seasons*, 53.

12   Balmain, *My Years and Seasons*, 33.

13   Balmain, *My Years and Seasons*, 63.

14 Balmain, *My Years and Seasons*, 64.

15 Balmain, *My Years and Seasons*, 68.

16 Balmain, *My Years and Seasons*, 67–68.

17 Press Kit for Pierre Balmain Spring Collection, 1976.

18 Press Kit for Pierre Balmain Spring Collection, 1976.

19 Press Kit for Pierre Balmain Spring Collection, 1976.

20 Balmain, *My Years and Seasons*, 3.

21 Balmain, *My Years and Seasons*, 21.

22 Balmain, *My Years and Seasons*, 22.

23 Balmain, "Des rapports de l'Architecture avec la Couture," 14.

24 Balmain, "Des rapports de l'Architecture avec la Couture," 13.

25 Balmain, "Des rapports de l'Architecture avec la Couture," 12.

26 Balmain, "Des rapports de l'Architecture avec la Couture," 13.

27 Balmain, "Des rapports de l'Architecture avec la Couture," 13.

28 Madame Alexandre, "Festival du Cinéma de Berlin," May 2, 1958, typewritten manuscript. Centre de Documentation Mode at the Musée des Arts Décoratifs.

29 Madame Alexandre, "Festival du Cinéma de Berlin," May 2, 1958

30 Balmain, "Des rapports de l'Architecture avec la Couture," 3.

31 Press Kit for Pierre Balmain Spring Collection, 1976.

32 Balmain, "Des rapports de l'Architecture avec la Couture," 8–9.

33 *Haute Couture Pierre Balmain—Erik Mortensen—Créations Contemporaines—Dessins de René Gruau,* exhibition brochure (Nantes: Galerie des Beaux-Arts, 1987).

34 "Pierre Balmain: 40 années de création au musée," *Le Courrier Picard*, January 23, 1986.

35 Hélène de Turckheim, "La mort de Pierre Balmain—Un Homme de raffinement," *Le Figaro*, June 30, 1982.

36 Janie Samet, "Le Couturier des années Rolls," *Le Figaro*, March 28, 1996.

37 Balmain, *My Years and Seasons*, 37.

38 Pierre Balmain, "Quelques mots de Pierre Balmain," *La Femme Chic*, no. 466, 1956, 148.

39 Balmain, *My Years and Seasons*, 36.

40 Laurence Beurdeley, "Il habillait les reines et Brigitte Bardot," *France Soir*, June 29, 1982.

41 Beurdeley, "Il habillait les reines et Brigitte Bardot."

42 *Haute Couture Pierre Balmain—Erik Mortensen—Créations Contemporaines—Dessins de René Gruau,* 1987.

43 Martine Leventer, "Pierre Balmain: la retouche," *Le Point*, January 26, 1976, 73.

44 Press Kit for Pierre Balmain Spring Collection, 1976.

YVES SAINT LAURENT

Monsieur Saint Laurent, you requested that we begin
this interview in a rather unconventional manner.

Let me read you something. I wrote it years ago, when I started making notes about my work. "There's something that has never been said, I think, that's very important. A woman who has not found her style, who is not at ease in her clothes, who does not live in harmony with herself, is an unhappy woman, unsure of herself; one could almost say she's ill. One speaks about the silence of health, the wonderful silence of health. One could also talk about the silence of clothing, the wonderful silence of clothing, that is the moment when the garment and the body are one, when one forgets completely what one is wearing, where the garment doesn't speak, doesn't catch you, when one feels as good dressed as naked. That perfect relationship between body and clothing and spirit."[1]

*How would you describe your role
in making elegance more accessible?*

After all these years of exploring, my art continues to fascinate me.
I know no greater joy. You think you've come to the end of the road,
you believe that everything is behind you — and suddenly you realize
that your perspectives are endless. Prior experience reveals these
perspectives to you. How many times have I felt helpless, shattered,
and desperate when blocked by the black curtain of despon-
dency — and how many times has that curtain been yanked away,
revealing to my eyes limitless horizons? At those moments, joy
and — dare I admit it? — flashes of true pride overtake me.[2]

Your profession has also caused you great distress, however.

My work preys on me. Creation is painful. All year round I am terrified. I live like a hermit. I don't go out. It's a hard life, which is why
I feel so close to Proust. I deeply admire all he has written about artistic
creation and its attendant miseries. I remember a sentence from
In the Shadow of Young Girls in Flower: "What wellspring of pain
had given him such unlimited creative powers?" I could quote other
magnificent passages from Proust, in which he touches on that same
kind of suffering. I copied out some of them, and had them framed
and nailed to the wall above my desk on avenue Marceau.[3] I know
that, for many long years, I did my work rigorously and honestly. . .
I fought for elegance and beauty. Every man needs aesthetic ghosts
in order to live. I have pursued them, sought them, hunted them
down. I have experienced many forms of anxiety, many forms of hell.
I have known fear and terrible solitude, the false friendship of tranquil-
izers and drugs, the prison of depression and mental homes. I emerged
from all that one day, dazzled but sober. Marcel Proust taught me
about neurotics, "that splendid and pitiable family which is the salt
of the earth." Without knowing it, I belonged to that family. I didn't
choose this fatal lineage, yet it is what allowed me to fly so high in
the sky of artistic creation, rub shoulders with Rimbaud's "makers
of fire," find myself, and understand that the greatest encounter of
one's life is the encounter with oneself.[4]

Why is being a couturier such a demanding profession?

Because it is terrifying. You lose extraordinary amounts of thinking power. It can be quite depressing. There are loads of things that escape you, things you'd like to do that you will never do. I would have liked to draw, to be in a theater company such as the "Living Theatre" for example . . . Unfortunately, you become a prisoner of your profession, of your success, of your talent. I don't like myself; quite the opposite: at times I realize that I have yet to escape "fashion" and "couture." I hope the profession changes. I hope that coming generations will transform it, and that one day fashion-show madness and tyrannical critics will disappear forever. And that stereotypes will be destroyed, as they have been in other fields.[5]

After all these years, is designing still a challenge for you?

Couture is a profession that demands enormous sacrifices. Each season, four times a year, you are faced with yourself, yes. Nothing is ever a given. I have been meeting these challenges for twenty-five years.[6] Each time I show a new collection, I have terrible stage fright, which is normal. I feel . . . the weight of responsibility; it is overwhelming: if I fail, several hundred people will be out of work. I rebel. I feel frustrated. I was never free to be young and happy-go-lucky.[7]

It sounds as though being a designer has made you painfully introspective.

Finding yourself means having pitiless clarity, knowing how hard you can look at yourself in order to know yourself better — though not so hard that you hate yourself.[8] I have had several eras; I don't regret any of them. Whatever happens, I am "always ready." There exist thousands of ways of interpreting one's life and one's profession. If changes occur in my profession, I imagine that they will be exciting, and fresh.[9]

Currently, your profession does seem to be undergoing changes.

Well, that's life. There are tendencies that fashion cannot escape. I think that, no matter what happens, the great designers will survive. But the lesser houses, which are not headed by great designers, will collapse. Now, snobbishness might have something to do with it; in some cases without a doubt. Be that as it may, quality always wins the day.[10]

Where is fashion headed?

Toward the coexistence of contradictions. On the one hand basic, almost asexual clothes for active life: sweaters, pants, trench-coats, safari jackets; the blouse dress for women. And then on the other hand evening clothes to seduce. Those I see as being ephemeral and unpredictable.[11] This change — that I hope will occur — began fifty years ago. And don't think for a minute that it will come about through the lengthening or shortening of dresses, or all the comments that people might make about that, nor through the more or less unexpected strangeness of line and form. No, no! I am talking about a spiritual revolution. People don't care about being elegant anymore; they want to seduce.[12]

How did you start out?

I sent my sketches to Michel de Brunhoff [editor in chief of *Vogue* France from 1929 to 1954], and he suggested an internship at the École du Syndicat de la Couture Parisienne. I could draw, but I knew nothing about the cut. That is where I learned about it . . . Well, let's say I got an inkling about it! Once I graduated from the École, Jean Cocteau and Christian Bérard introduced me to Christian Dior. It was a wonderful opportunity for me. I could go on working in couture (for I must admit that I have always been absolutely incapable of doing anything I don't like)![13]

*Is it an exaggeration to say that meeting
Christian Dior changed your life forever?*

Working with Christian Dior was, for me, nothing short of miraculous.
My admiration for him knew no bounds. He was the most celebrated
couturier of the time; he had created a unique house; he had an exceptional staff; he was a maestro. He taught me the fundamentals.[14]

Do you remember your first encounter with him?

I was a provincial lad, still wet behind the ears, and he fascinated me.
I was very intimidated, so I didn't say a word. You can't imagine what
fashion was at that time. Ah, the opulence of the Maison Dior![15]

*When he died suddenly in October 1957,
you were named his successor.*

I had already become extremely important chez Dior. Two months
before dying, he said to my mother, "I have found my heir; Yves will
take over when I'm gone."[16] When I was working chez Dior, and
Monsieur Dior was still alive, I made my mother's dresses. I made her
a dress in black organza, and another in gray and white taffeta; I made
her a gray suit with an Italian straw hat, and so many other things.
Thinking back on my New Look period, I see my mother in a light blue
summer suit, with a huge pleated skirt. She is wearing a canotier, a rose
around her neck, a black velvet ribbon, and a flounce around her waist.
I even painted her portrait wearing that suit. I liked to paint then.[17]
When Christian Dior passed away, I had the opportunity to present
and create my own collections. . . At the age of twenty-one I entered
a celebrity fortress from which I have yet to escape. I will always love
theater, but Dior taught me — more than fashion or design — to love
the fundamental nobility of the profession of couturier.[18]

Your appointment did not meet with unanimous approval.

Especially within Dior's main backer: the Boussac group. They didn't
believe that a boy my age could replace Christian Dior. But Raymonde
Zehnacker, his éminence grise, managed to convince them.[19]

The very first show was a great success.
What was the secret of that collection?

Very simple: I lightened Monsieur Dior's clothes. I removed
the padding, the toile, the corset.[20]

Then in 1960 the rug was pulled out from under you
when you were called up for military service.

It was a terrible experience. It was like going back to school. I told them
I was having a nervous breakdown, so they sent me to the hospital.
After two weeks, the doctors gathered and decided to cut me loose.
But then, Pierre Messmer, who was minister of the armed forces,
retracted their decision. It was during the Algerian War and Marcel
Boussac didn't want anyone to be able to say that he was protecting
me. So they sent me to the Hôpital du Val-de-Grâce. I stayed there
two and a half months. . . It was a nightmare. To prevent me from
leaving they knocked me out with medication. I was in bed in a room,
alone, with people constantly coming and going. Crazy people.
Bona fide lunatics. Some of them would fondle me. I protested.
Others screamed for no reason at all. Everything you need to produce
anxiety. I was so scared that during the entire time I was there, two
and a half months, I only went to the bathroom once. By the end
I must have weighed eighty pounds. My brain was mush.[21]

Tell us more about your depression and the
relapses frequently reported in the press.

Pierre Bergé is undoubtedly correct when he says that I was born
depressed. I am both strong and weak.[22]

You are the most Parisian of couturiers,
yet you were born and grew up in North Africa.

Our world at the time was Oran, and not Paris. Nor Algiers, Camus'
metaphysical city, nor Marrakech and her benevolent pink magic.
Oran, a cosmopolitan town made up of people from all over, and
mostly from abroad, a glittering city, a patchwork of a thousand
colors under the calm North African sun.[23]

It was a good place to be well off, and we were well off.[24]
Like colonials elsewhere, like provincials, we maintained a lot of ties
to our roots.[25]

Where is your family from originally?

My father, who owned an insurance business and who was also
involved in a few movie productions, was descended from Alsatians
who had left Colmar, France when the Germans took it in 1870.
Lawyers, judges, notaries, they had worn the robe of public office.
One of my ancestors wrote the marriage contract between Napoléon
and Josephine and was made a baron for it.[26]

Would it be accurate to say that you had a happy childhood?

Yes. There was my mother, naturally, my two sisters, who were younger
than I, my grandmother and my great-aunt. We lived in Oran in a large
four-story house and we were a very joyous family. However, I began
to lead a double life in grade school: on the one hand there was the joy
that reigned in our house and the imaginary world I conjured up with
my drawings, stage sets, costumes, and theater; and on the other
the Catholic school I attended, a world from which, as a pensive,
shy dreamer, I found myself excluded and where my schoolmates
mocked and terrorized and beat me. During recess I hid in the church,
and when the final bell rang, I waited for all my classmates to depart
before leaving myself, to avoid their abuse. It was around that time that
I became determined to conquer Paris and climb as far up the ladder as
I could. Inwardly, I told my classmates that I was going to get revenge:
they would grow up and be nothing, and I would be everything.
I didn't mention to anyone, not even my mother, what they made me
endure at school. As soon as I got home I went to my room and drew
little silhouettes on a piece of cardboard (a little over six inches high)
that I would cut out and dress with costumes of real cloth, and that
in one fell swoop became both my models and my characters. I had
a room all to myself in which to do this; I built myself a box four
and a half feet high, and made stage settings, and did the lighting,
and basically recreated an entire theatrical experience.[27]

*Was there a pivotal moment during your
teenage years that left a mark on you?*

In 1949, when I was thirteen I saw *L'École des femmes* directed
by Louis Jouvet, with stage sets by Christian Bérard. Bérard's power
immediately floored me. He made me even more resolute in my desire
to pursue my calling. I wanted to be set designer like him. Bérard knew
how to bring a character to life; he knew how to build a costume, by
reinventing it with the purest of lines... As soon as I got home I wanted
to do *L'École des femmes* over again. My mother gave me an old bed
sheet. I dyed it several colors using gouaches, and cut it to pieces to
dress my little characters. My sisters and cousins watched the perfor-
mance. I did all the voices.[28]

You already knew you wanted to be famous.

I was always very ambitious. I can't hide that. Very, very young
I already wanted to be somebody, to show what I could do. When
I was ten, at a birthday party, I said to my whole family: "One day,
my name will be written in letters of fire on the Champs-Élysées."
And it's very funny because there is a Saint Laurent boutique on
the Champs-Élysées. It's a kid's dream, really. But you mustn't see
pride in that.[29]

Your mother, Lucienne, was your first muse, was she not?

My mother was a well-dressed woman. She liked to go out, and when
she went dancing we children would follow her, marveling at her
beauty as she awaited our goodnight kisses. A white tulle dress with
big sleeves and large white polka-dots comes to mind, and it does
so poetically — the tulle is so light, so spiderlike. Years later, at Dior
I designed a dress similar to that one. I have another vivid memory
of how the seed of my 1940s collection — which the critics panned
— was planted.

This was during the war. We were in the outskirts of Oran, in the country. My father was not there that day, and my mother ran away — she went to a dance at the American military base. We children followed her in secret, along with the servants. We wanted to see our mother dance. The windows were high, so one of the servants picked me up in his arms and I was able to see my mother on the dance floor. She was wearing a black crepe dress that ended just above the knees with short sleeves and a V neckline. She had pinned on a bouquet of daisies, cornflowers, and poppies, and in lieu of a necklace she wore a plastic cross on a black velvet ribbon. Exquisite. My 1940 collection is a direct copy of that.[30]

*Your hometown of Oran appears to have had
quite an influence both on your imagination
and on your future inspirations.*

The intense melting pot of lives I knew in Oran as a child during
the war marked me. North Africa was a strategic place.[31]

Is creativity always inspired by the past?

Every creation is in fact a recreation, a new way of looking at the
same old things, expressing them differently, bringing them into
closer focus, highlighting an angle that somehow previously had
escaped notice, and emphasizing forms.[32]

*Was your famous safari jacket directly inspired
by the uniforms you saw at the time?*

It was the uniform the Allies wore, in khaki and beige. Then there was
navy blue, and the white uniforms of the navy officers. Oran was a big
port, there were warships. People tried to have some glamour in their
lives because they were close to death. I sill love ports, I'm fascinated
by Rio de Janeiro, Singapore, New York of course, Marseille, Hong
Kong. That whole traffic of boats.[33]

Did your peasant blouses also stem from your past in Oran?

That was my childhood. I spent my holidays with my grandparents,
who had some property inland from Oran, vineyards. There was a
kind of Atlanta feeling about it — women working in the vines with
big scarves on their heads, peasant blouses with gathered skirts.
None of that has changed.[34]

*What about the female version of the tuxedo?
Where did that come from?*

I was deeply struck by a photograph of Marlene Dietrich wearing
men's clothes. A tuxedo, a blazer, or a naval-officer's uniform
— any of them. A woman dressed as a man must be at the height
of her femininity to fight against a costume that isn't hers.
She should be wonderfully made up and refined in every detail.[35]

What is fashion's take on sexual roles and perceptions?

Virility is no longer linked to gray flannel and muscular shoulders, nor
is femininity still beholden to chiffon or plunging necklines. I think the
time of baby doll women and dominant males is over. Girls don't need
to simper anymore, or play stupid and show their legs to signal that they
are women. The boys don't need to bang on the floor with their canes,
to prance and wax their moustaches to prove that they are men. Before,
men and women were different planets that would come into each other's
orbits once in a while. Today, boys and girls are better than equal: they can
be close while remaining different. There is more tenderness nowadays;
they are more sincere and don't give a damn about traditional imagery.
Since they lead the same lives, it is normal that they should wear the same
jeans, the same sweaters, the same sailor's shirts, the same tunics.[36]

Black veils have been prominent throughout your career.

Black veils always come back in my collections, it's the idea of death
— when a collection is over, it doesn't belong to me anymore, and I die
a little with it. And maybe too it's the Arab veil. The idea of veils of black
chiffon or black tulle is almost a physical presence with me. It's mystery.[37]

Black has several layers of meaning for you.

I like black because it is assertive, it emphasizes, it stylizes . . . I always
light it up with gold, with buttons, with belts, with chains. I highlight it
with very long, fluttering, white scarves. I don't like to see women
wearing my suits with blouses; a simple T-shirt is better. Black also looks
good in the sun. I hate bright colors when it's sunny out: yellow, orange,
pink, turquoise — it's too easy. For those ladies who dislike black, there
is navy blue. And if you like to change from time to time, try white with
natural, sandy, earthy colors.[38]

You have been using black since the very beginning.

For my first collections I often expressed myself in black. Large black lines
symbolized the pencil stroke on the white page, that is to say the purest,
most perfect line. I started with black; then I worked my way through
other dark colors, except for red, which I have always loved passionately.[39]

What does red bring to the table?

Red is the basis of makeup: lipstick, nail polish. Red is a noble color; rubies are red; it's a dangerous color. Sometimes you have to flirt with danger. Red is religious, it is blood, it is royal, it is Phaedra and a multitude of heroines. Red is like a battle between life and death.[40]

You are known for striking color schemes.

Well, that is really because of a certain evolution in my profession. I was more comfortable with dark colors because they hid a weakness of mine. Now that I am better at what I do, I am much more daring in my use of colors.[41]

Your stylistic vocabulary is based on certain recurring themes and variations.

They are large baroque themes. I have been carrying them around within me for a long time. For example, I have always been extremely sensitive to painters. To Matisse. To Mondrian. To Picasso. I based some of my dresses on their paintings. To Fernand Léger. And then there are the clothes that were inspired by ethnic fashions . . . Is that the correct term? In Africa, in Asia, and in the Slavic countries, clothes don't evolve much, and most of the time young women wear the same dresses as old women. Which goes to prove my theory that you can wear whatever you want at any age. It might also explain the uniformity of my men's clothing line. The jacket can be navy blue or white or black. A tuxedo can be worn with a long skirt, a short skirt, or pants. You can create variations on these themes, which, it must be said, ensured my success and thanks to which Chanel at one time considered me a kind of successor. She thought I was on the right track.[42]

Did you spend time with Mademoiselle Chanel?

No. I was afraid to get to know her. She intimidated me terribly. I only met her once, at the Ritz. I was obliged to go and say hello. I was with Lauren Bacall, who was wearing a miniskirt, and as we all know, Chanel did not approve of miniskirts. Chanel said to me, "Whatever you do, Saint Laurent, no miniskirts."[43]

Could you describe your creative method?

I follow the same process as a painter, a sculptor, an architect, a musician. A couturier's creative process aims to invent a fashion. It's daring to be original, like Chanel, Balenciaga, Dior; in brief, it's finding and imposing a style. In 1960 I was lucky, but one could never say that I had a style.

But finding a style is not enough. You have to assert it, hone it, rejuvenate it. Nowadays, for example, I can make a jacket four times a year, and it'll be different each time. Perfecting essential articles of clothing — what a wonderful job — is how I became who I am; it is what allowed me to go beyond fashion; and it is why women can wear very old dresses of mine and never feel like they are outdated.[44] At the beginning of each month that corresponds to the year's four collections, I have no time to myself. I feel like a prisoner. I am empty. And then one day everything changes, and I become the happiest of couturiers. I watch this man jumping around and working, who has ideas and intuitions, and whose exploits bowl me over. Alas, I am alone when I fail, but there are always two of me when I am successful.[45]

I make a lot of mistakes. I waste a lot when I work. Then I proceed by process of elimination. Every three days I have a studio presentation, and I cut several designs each time. I end up with very little, following Charlie Chaplin's advice: "Shake the tree and keep only what holds fast to the branches." Before, my sketches were a starting-off point. That's the biggest mistake you can make. Nothing is better if you want to imprison yourself in a system. I learned to be highly suspicious of inspiration, and little by little I understood that couture is not an art, but a craft, that is to say that its point of departure and its goal is physical: a woman's body, and not a bunch of abstract ideas that might have some kind of intrinsic interest. A dress is not "architecture," it's a house: it does not exist to be looked at, but to be lived in, and the woman who inhabits it should feel beautiful and comfortable in it. The rest is just idle chatter.[46]

What are the challenges you face?

The thing I will never learn to master is my inability to believe in my own imagination and inventiveness. I will always think that all is lost; I know that. The other thing I will never be able to shake — much like the fear of beginning — is the sadness, the emptiness of the end. I imagine it must feel the same way when you write a book. When it is all over, when the last pin is put into place, you feel like an orphan. All your ideas have been used and are dead; they disappear like those that preceded them, and like the ones that are upcoming. Nothing will remain of all that effort, all those sleepless nights . . . That is cruel. To bring forth things that you will never see again and whose very essence requires that they disappear. Fashion is inherently ephemeral.[47]

How long does it take to master the couture profession?

It probably takes about fifteen years to get a sixth sense about what you are doing.[48]

Are you generally alone when you create?

This profession is rooted in passion: besides me, a man who ceases to live when things are not going his way, and who is never satisfied with anything until the day of the show, there are the seamstresses. They work by hand; they are the keepers of the secrets of *grande couture* (which their mothers and grandmothers taught them). There are these *couturières* whose craft is disappearing, and who will no longer have a raison d'être in the society of the future, and then there are the women who spend their days and nights at the sewing machine. Often I make them rip apart what they have been doing, but I never disrespect them: I never have them work on something I don't believe in myself; they would feel it, and have contempt for me. When the creative process begins, standing in my atelier, giving my various teams order upon order and assigning them task upon task and not knowing myself if all this bustle and all this frenzied work will lead me where I want to go, I feel alone. At that moment everyone needs me, and looks to me, waiting for me to tell them what to do, and I feel responsible for each and every one of them.[49]

Is the creative process easy for you?

Certain years were very tough. I sometimes didn't come up with the theme or the idea until ten days before the show, and during those ten days everybody lost their minds. Then I would show up, exhausted, facing all these women looking at me, often with sympathy, but with more than a touch of severity.[50]

How do you design your dresses?

All of my dresses are born out of movement. A dress that does not reflect or make you think of movement is not a good dress. Once you have found the movement you've been seeking, then you can choose the color, the form, the fabric — not before. For example, there is the straight cut and the bias cut. For years I was partial to the straight cut, because it fit my ideas. I knew the bias, of course, but I used it badly, a little like a composer unaware of the existence of sharp notes. I just couldn't "see" the bias. Then, three years ago a woman came to see me. She taught me everything about the bias. That was the year, you might remember, when all my dresses were folkloric, puffy, Russian, and so on. It's just that I had learned to cut on the bias. It was not a journey all the way to Russia, but a far more arduous journey. And I know that the sum of the artifices of this so-called artificial profession will always escape me.[51]

How important is a model to the creation of a dress?

For me, the model has a very important role to play. Without a living model, I could never create a dress, since there would be no life in it. In this I am very different from many couturiers who like to work on wooden mannequins. For my part, I can only work with live models, with living beings who inspire me. Without these women, nothing comes to me. I wrap them in fabric; I want to see how the material flows and plays on their bodies. These movements make want me to celebrate the moment with a quick sketch.[52]

I systematically look for girls who resemble the "it girls," the girls — or women — who personify their era. Catherine Deneuve for example. There is a woman who helped me a lot, a model called Danielle. She came from Lyon, and had worked very little in fashion. When I chose her I realized that her body, her gestures typified today's modern woman. Everything was there! I didn't need to teach her anything. On the contrary, she helped me to discard outdated references — the dust of couture. Something happened between us. I transformed her, no doubt, but her attitude, her behavior never varied. Whenever something I tried on her didn't work I knew I had to throw it out immediately and forever! She helped me improve.[53]

Are you ever frustrated by reactions to your collections?

People see only the trivial side of a collection. They never see the technique. They never see the work. They are obsessed with finding the gimmick, the formula. They say, "This year it's long or it's short or it's red or it's black." But they never grasp the general meaning. It escapes them totally.[54]

What is the secret to your success?

I think my success depends on my ability to tune in to the life of the moment even if I don't really live it.[55]

Have you had any failures?

Two resounding ones: . . . a sad collection that I brought out right at the moment when Courrèges was introducing his glorious miniskirts. When I see the photos I have a hard time believing I did that. It is not at all surprising that that collection was not successful. On the other hand I had a hard time swallowing the insults the international press hurled at me when I brought out . . . my 1940s collection. I never heard the end of the platform shoes, the frizzy red hair, the flowing dresses, below the knee, the silver fox fur All the girls adopted it.[56] Even those who didn't wear my clothes embraced that fashion. To this day, by the way . . . However, it also degenerated into the punk style that for me is the negation of fashion.[57]

*What do you see as your contribution
to the contemporary fashion vocabulary?*

I wanted to make a base that would be changeless, for a man and
for a woman. It was absolutely a conscious choice. I've noticed that
men were surer of themselves than women, because their clothes don't
change — just the color of the shirt and tie — while women were a
little abandoned, sometimes terrified, by a fashion that was coming
in, or fashion that was only for those under thirty. And I rebelled
against that, and since then I have tried every year to perfect a classic
style, and that's my safe place.[58]

In the end, you created the modern wardrobe.

I created the contemporary woman's wardrobe. I participated in changing my era. I did it with clothes, which is undoubtedly less important than music, or architecture, or painting, and many other arts, but be that as it may, I did it. I hope you will forgive me for being proud of what I did, but I have long believed that fashion exists not only to make women more beautiful, but also to give them confidence and faith in themselves. I have always been opposed to the fantasies of certain people who travel the world gratifying their egos through fashion. I have done quite the opposite: I put myself at the service of women. I served them. I served their bodies, their attitudes, their lives. I wanted to help them advance in the liberation movement that began in the last century.[59] As a designer, I never promoted "cosmic" clothes . . . And I don't see why one should change from one season to the next when the clothes are fine. Whether it be raincoats or blue jeans, tuxedos or trench-coats. This is why I ended up making the same models in ready-to-wear and in couture. The more a garment is perfect the more it is simple. I wasn't going to add buttons and pleats just to make it look rich![60]

What part of your profession do you like least?

I don't enjoy creating fashion on a fixed schedule. All those dresses that die in one year and, at the same time, all the other dresses that one must make. It's both a tomb and a womb. I feel torn between life and death, between past and future. Each time you have to question everything. You are never allowed to be wrong. You cannot afford to be right in three or four years. You are always dealing directly with the outside world.

A couturier is asked to feel everything that is going on and everything that will soon be going on, and to translate that. I made the rope with which to hang myself. I'd love to create fashion only when I felt like it, but I am bound by the financial empire I have spawned.[61]

What should a dress bring to the woman who wears it?

She is bearing a message! But its first goal is to make the woman
more attractive and comfortable in the garment. For me, elegance
is first and foremost forgetting totally what you are wearing.[62]

What makes the cocktail dress unique?

It is a couture tic. Let us say, an elegant dress. There is a space
to fill. Let's say a woman is going out and has nothing to wear.
Before, she had to make up for that lack by improvising.
Now, she has had enough. She is looking for something else.
The cocktail dress needs to be reinvented.[63]

Do you have a favorite design?

If I had to choose one design out of all those I have presented,
without a doubt it would be the tuxedo. It appeared on the scene
for the first time in 1966 with a transparent blouse and men's
trousers. And since then, the tuxedo has been featured every year
in my collections. In a way, it is the Yves Saint Laurent "label."[64]

If you had been able to invent a garment,
what would it have been?

I have often said that I wish I had invented blue jeans: the most
spectacular, the most practical, the most relaxed and nonchalant.
They have expression, modesty, sex appeal, simplicity — all I hope
for in my clothes.[65]

Do you consider fashion an art?

An art? I would rather say an artistic profession. It is extremely
complex, and varied. And it does resemble the creative process
of the painter, the sculptor, the theater director — since the fashion
show is such an important event. You must know how to choose
a dress that comes after the one you are looking at now. You risk
killing one dress with another.[66]

In a way, maturity turned me into a painter. More than the beauty of line, it is the relation to material that interested me. A rebellious, frightening material can be a terrible battleground; material that one must submit to the forces of the imagination. Like a river, my imagination has churned music, painting, sculpture, literature, and that thing that Nietzsche called the "aesthetic ghosts," without which life would not be worth living.[67]

In 1983 the prestigious Metropolitan Museum of Art presented a retrospective of your work, a first for a living couturier. How would you describe that experience?

It's awesome to see one's work gathered like that, those twenty-five years. I chose the dresses, and it was strange to find them again, and to see that they hadn't altered. Some of the clothes were things we'd kept back, others belonged to clients; and there was a choice of forty garments that Diana Vreeland had from Dior. What was most striking for me was this feeling that my clothes cannot get dated, which is after all the *réussite de ma vie* — the greatest satisfaction I have in my work, if not in my life.[68]

What did that experience teach you?

Preparing for the Metropolitan show was hard, I was very scared . . . One always says to oneself that maybe all one's work seen together will destroy a myth. I'm not astonished that the show is happening in America because America has always welcomed what I did, maybe because it's a new country, not loaded down with a whole big past. I've always had tremendous warmth from Americans.[69]

For decades now we've been hearing about the death of couture. How would you define couture today?

Couture is a multitude of whispered secrets. Few have the privilege of transmitting them.[70] It might be immoral or anachronistic to say so, but those dresses represent a very specific bit of work, which would simply be impossible to reproduce in ready-to-wear. Women who order them are, perhaps unintentionally, acting as patrons. When couture dies, it will mark the end of one of the great human crafts.[71]

*Who are the women today who have managed
to impose a signature style?*

Female style-setters are few and far between. First of all, there are
many different groups, different constituencies, each with its own
style. There are many different lifestyles within the same society.
There used to be only two groups: high society people and everybody
else. Today there are a thousand different groups. The intelligent thing
I think is to mix everything up, and draw from all the possibilities.[72]

What is the first thing you look at in a woman?

I attach more importance to the movement of a body than to the
way it is dressed. Some women can be dressed in a perfectly ordinary
way and be very elegant and extraordinary, if only by their personalities and their gestures.[73]

How important is a woman's age?

What makes a woman old is not her wrinkles, nor her white hair. It is
her movements. Which is where accessories are crucial. My accessories
are movements. A scarf you can play with, a shoulder bag that frees up
the hands — nothing is more ugly than a bag held at arm's length. A soft
belt — always with a chain — that allows you to sway your hips; and
pockets. Pockets are very important. Take two women both wearing
a tube jersey. The one with pockets will immediately feel superior to
the other. Letting your arms hang down or being obliged to cross them
or to fiddle with your wedding ring: these movements are ungainly,
they are handicaps. Then there are the shoes. Shoes should never slow
you down; they should bring a spring to your step.[74]

Should women be idolized?

My idea of a woman is an object of worship, and I'm thinking not
only in the holy sense, but also as something to be covered in gold,
the way the conquistadors adorned statues of the Virgin with
booty — covering her with gold and presents.[75]

In 2002 you made the difficult decision to close your house.
In the history of fashion, only Cristóbal Balenciaga had had
the courage to do that at the height of his fame.

I was lucky enough to become, at eighteen, Christian Dior's assistant, to take over from him at twenty-one, and encounter success with my very first collection in 1958. Soon it will be forty-four years. All those years I lived only for and through my job. And yet, I have chosen to walk away from the profession I loved so much. I also say goodbye to the aesthetic ghosts that haunted me all these years. I have known them since childhood and this marvelous profession has allowed me to keep them close. Thanks to them I was able to gather round me a family that has helped and protected me immeasurably. This family is mine and one can well imagine how painful it is for me right now to leave this family since I know that Paradise is never more delightful than when lost. I want them to know that they will always be in my heart — that for more than forty years has beat in time with my house.[76]

Any advice for young designers starting out in fashion?

Don't burn your wings on the flames of fashion.[77]

Define luxury.

Luxury is above all an attitude of the heart. I never considered it something that revolves around money, jewels, or furs: it's mostly respect for others.[78]

Any thoughts on contemporary fashion?

I am very worried about the turn fashion has taken: all show and not enough content. I dreamed the other night that Chanel and I went for dinner at the Ritz and when we passed in front of rue Cambon we both began to cry.[79]

*You wanted to be famous from a very young age;
your dream came true. What has fame brought you?*

I like fame. I like it. It's festive. I love parties. It's happy. It sparkles.
It glitters. It's bubbly. Champagne. Gold candelabras, gold paneling,
gold decorations. Fame is always golden. Gold leaf. It's old. It's secular.
It's noisy — very noisy. It's explosive. It's like lightning. It can't be
bothered. It walks all over you. It disturbs the peace. I wanted fame
and fortune. Fame gives me strength. It cleanses and purifies me.
It embalms me. I am a crucified effigy on the chest of that queenly
heroine, that goddess we call fame.[80]

A parting adage for our readers?

The great art, Prince Metternich said, is to last.[81]

NOTES

1 Joan Juliet Buck, "Yves Saint Laurent on Style, Passion, and Beauty," *Vogue*, December 1983, 300.

2 Yves Saint Laurent, *Yves Saint Laurent par Yves Saint Laurent* (Paris: Editions Herscher, 1986), 27.

3 Yvonne Baby, "Yves Saint Laurent au Met: Portrait de l'artiste," *Le Monde*, December 8, 1983, 29.

4 Yves Saint Laurent's farewell address at 5 avenue Marceau, January 7, 2002, typescript. Fondation Pierre Bergé-Yves Saint Laurent, Paris.

5 Philippe Labro "Yves Saint Laurent: La mode d'aujourd'hui c'est démodé," *Le Journal du Dimanche*, February 2, 1969.

6 Jean-François Josselin, "Les années Saint Laurent," *Le Nouvel Observateur*, December 1983, 59.

7   Claude Berthod, "Saint-Laurent coupez pour nous," *Elle* (France), March 1968, 95.

8   Buck, "Yves Saint Laurent on Style, Passion, and Beauty," 396.

9   Baby, "Yves Saint Laurent au Met: Portrait de l'artiste."

10 Claude Cézan, *La mode, phénomène humain* (Paris: Privat, 1967), 131.

11 Claude Berthod, "L'événement-mode de la rentrée: Yves Saint Laurent choisit le prêt à porter," *Elle* (France), September 1971, 10 — 11.

12 Cézan, 130.

13 Cézan, 131.

14 Saint Laurent, *Yves Saint Laurent par Yves Saint Laurent*, 15.

15 Barbara Schwarm and Martine Leventer, "Yves Saint Laurent: Roi de la mode," *Le Point*, July 1977, 52.

16 Schwarm and Leventer, "Yves Saint Laurent: Roi de la mode," 52.

17 Baby, "Yves Saint Laurent au Met: Portrait de l'artiste."

18 Saint Laurent, *Yves Saint Laurent par Yves Saint Laurent*, 15–16.

19 Frantz-Olivier Giesbert and Janie Samet, "Yves Saint Laurent: Je suis né avec une dépression nerveuse . . .," *Le Figaro*, July 11, 1991.

20 Giesbert and Samet, "Yves Saint Laurent: Je suis né avec une dépression nerveuse . . ."

21 Giesbert and Samet, "Yves Saint Laurent: Je suis né avec une dépression nerveuse . . ."

22 Giesbert and Samet, "Yves Saint Laurent: Je suis né avec une dépression nerveuse . . ."

23 Yves Saint Laurent, *Yves Saint Laurent*, New York: The Metropolitan Museum of Art, December 14, 1983–September 2, 1984, 15.

24 Yves Saint Laurent, *Yves Saint Laurent*, 15.

25 Yves Saint Laurent, *Yves Saint Laurent*, 15.

26 Yves Saint Laurent, *Yves Saint Laurent*, 15.

27 Baby, "Yves Saint Laurent au Met: Portrait de l'artiste."

28 Baby, "Yves Saint Laurent au Met: Portrait de l'artiste."

29 Buck, "Yves Saint Laurent on Style, Passion, and Beauty," 396.

30 Baby, "Yves Saint Laurent au Met: Portrait de l'artiste."

31 Buck, "Yves Saint Laurent on Style, Passion, and Beauty," 300.

32 David Teboul, *Yves Saint Laurent 5 avenue Marceau 75116 Paris, France* (Paris: Éditions de La Martinière, 2002).

33 Buck, "Yves Saint Laurent on Style, Passion, and Beauty," 300.

34 Buck, "Yves Saint Laurent on Style, Passion, and Beauty," 300.

35 Yves Saint Laurent, *Yves Saint Laurent par Yves Saint Laurent*, 20–21.

36 Claude Berthod, "Les hommes nouveaux que nous prépare Saint Laurent," *Elle* (France), May 1969, 154.

37 Buck, "Yves Saint Laurent on Style, Passion, and Beauty," 301.

38 Yves Saint Laurent, *Yves Saint Laurent par Yves Saint Laurent*, 96–97.

39 Baby, "Yves Saint Laurent au Met: Portrait de l'artiste."

40 Baby, "Yves Saint Laurent au Met: Portrait de l'artiste."

41 Hélène de Turckheim, "Saint Laurent dessine son 'été 34' et répond aux questions," *Le Figaro*, October 16, 1973.

42 Josselin, "Les années Saint Laurent," 58.

43 Giesbert and Samet, "Yves Saint Laurent: Je suis né avec une dépression nerveuse ..."

44 Baby, "Yves Saint Laurent au Met: Portrait de l'artiste."

45 Françoise Sagan, "Saint Laurent par Françoise Sagan," *Elle* (France), March 3, 1980, 9, 12.

46 Berthod, "Saint Laurent coupez pour nous," 95.

47 Sagan, "Saint Laurent par Françoise Sagan," 12 .

48 Buck, "Yves Saint Laurent on Style, Passion, and Beauty," 301.

49 Sagan, "Saint Laurent par Françoise Sagan," 9.

50 Sagan, "Saint Laurent par Françoise Sagan," 9.

51 Sagan, "Saint Laurent par Françoise Sagan," 12.

52 Josselin, "Les années Saint Laurent," 58.

53 Labro, "La mode d'aujourd'hui c'est démodé."

54 Labro, "La mode d'aujourd'hui c'est démodé."

55 Barbara Rose, "The Intimate Yves," *Vogue*, October 1978, 404.

56 Turckheim, "Saint Laurent dessine son 'été 34' et répond aux questions."

57 Josselin, "Les années Saint Laurent," 59.

58 Buck, "Yves Saint Laurent on Style, Passion, and Beauty," 301.

59 Yves Saint Laurent's farewell address, January 7, 2002.

60 Berthod, "L'événement-mode de la rentrée: Yves Saint Laurent choisit le prêt à porter," 8.

61 Schwarm and Leventer, "Yves Saint Laurent: Roi de la mode," 57.

62 Josselin, "Les années Saint Laurent," 58.

63 "Yves Saint Laurent: A Nous Deux le Prêt-A-Porter," *Gap*, November 1971, 26.

64 Iréne Vacher, "Catherine Deneuve et Helmut Newton: La grande revue des 20 ans Saint-Lauren," *ParisMatch,* December 4, 1981, 64.

65 Saint Laurent, *Yves Saint Laurent*, 23–24.

66 Josselin, "Les années Saint Laurent," 58.

67 Yves Saint Laurent, preface to *Histoire technique & morale du Vêtement*, Maguelonne Toussaint-Samat (Paris: Editions Bordas, 1990).

68 Buck, "Yves Saint Laurent on Style, Passion, and Beauty," 396.

69 Buck, "Yves Saint Laurent on Style, Passion, and Beauty," 396.

70 Teboul, *Yves Saint Laurent*.

71 Berthod, "L'événement-mode de la rentrée: Yves Saint Laurent choisit le prêt à porter," 10.

72 Rose, "The Intimate Yves," 407.

73 Buck, "Yves Saint Laurent on Style, Passion, and Beauty," *Vogue* (US), December 1983, 301.

74 Berthod, "Saint Laurent coupez pour nous," 97.

75 Buck, "Yves Saint Laurent on Style, Passion, and Beauty," 301.

76 Yves Saint Laurent's farewell address, January 7, 2002.

77 Teboul, *Yves Saint Laurent*.

78 Barbara Rose, "The Intimate Yves", *Vogue* US, October 1978, 404.

79 Janie Samet, "Saint Laurent a choisi la liberté," *Le Figaro*, September 15, 1994.

80 Giesbert and Samet, "Yves Saint Laurent: Je suis né avec une dépression nerveuse ..."

81 Saint Laurent, *Yves Saint Laurent*, 24.

ALEXANDER MCQUEEN

Alexander McQueen, you can't seem to shake the "fashion hooligan" tag.

Everywhere I go it's the same thing! Even when I was still a student we were all labeled. We were all supposedly "Saint-Martinists" or "Gallianoists." I hate being pigeonholed, being compared to other people.[1] I just don't like being labeled. At the end of the day you're an individual.[2] I'm not this *enfant terrible*, or whatever it is — stupid word . . . I'm not like that at all, but sometimes I act like that.[3]

*Does it still bother you after all these years,
or have you gotten used to it?*

It's funny that journalists continue to portray me as a bad boy,
when I'm too old to be considered a boy anymore. That being said,
it's a journalist thing. I imagine Gaultier must find it amusing to still
be labeled "fashion's enfant terrible" thirty years on. I think the misun-
derstanding stems from my first interviews. I am not eloquent by nature,
and was even less so early on in my career. This is because of my background. I grew up in a non-verbal environment. So I was often misquoted
in articles about me. Also, I don't like explaining myself. For that matter,
I don't stick around backstage after my shows attempting to decode
my supposed message for journalists. My guiding principle is that my
work speaks for itself.[4]

*And yet you are known for being, shall we say,
impulsive, are you not?*

I remember after one show an Italian journalist asked me why I was
so aggressive. I said, "Fuck off! Can't you see what kind of world
we live in? What's going on around us? If I'm aggressive, that's just
the way it is. It's my state of mind at a given moment. It's not pre-
meditated. Period."[5]

*Fashion design has never been an easy career choice.
Is that still the case today?*

This hasn't happened overnight. I've been in the business since
I was sixteen and my style is still evolving. Sooner or later I'll find
my niche and try to evolve it more productively.[6]

Why did you choose this line of work?

I became a designer to push new ideas. I don't see the point of
designing something that's already been done twenty million
different ways.[7] I do this job because it's the only job I know
how to do. It's kind of sad.[8] It's an industry that doesn't believe
in giving, just taking.[9]

What would you have liked to do instead?

I always wanted to be an architect but I'm not intelligent enough. I couldn't do the math.[10]

In the 1990s there was a huge wave of British designers arriving to work in Paris. Seeing as you were at the forefront of this movement, can you explain how it came about?

British fashion is known for projecting forward and that is what they are looking for. The British fashion industry is the best in the world for turning out designers. It always has been from the year dot. Charles Worth was English and he was the first person to do couture in Paris.[11] I also think that the thing that makes us English designers popular is that we have the balls to assert our independence.[12]

You are often mentioned in the same breath as another Brit — John Galliano. What is the major difference between your respective styles?

John's a hopeless romantic and I've become a hopeless realist, but you need both in the world.[13]

At one time you were based in Paris and were staging shows in New York. Outside of their being inescapable in the fashion world, what are the similarities between the two cities?

New York has this very brash image but then the clothing is so conservative. I think it's good to bring a little excitement to New York fashion week, because it always has a lot of buzz around it because of the celebrities . . .[14] I've never fit into Paris. I can't get into that superstar lifestyle, I just can't. I think I've tried to mingle. I've been out to dinner with John [Galliano]; I've had dinner with Madonna. But it's just not my world. We just don't fit properly.[15]

Can a fashion designer claim to be an artist?

I am a craftsman.[16] I am not an artist. I'm selling a service.[17]

Okay, another trick question: Do you believe
that fashion is an art in its own right?

I don't. But I like to break down barriers. It's not a specific way of thinking; it's just what's in my mind at the time.[18] There's an intellectual input, of course, but you should be able to work it out yourself. Clothes don't come with a notepad. It's eclectic. It comes from Degas and Monet and my sister-in-law in Dagenham.[19]

Apparently, you've never been reluctant
to mix commercialism and design.

I think the word "commercialism" has got this gray cloud over it, but I don't think it's a bad word. You can have spontaneity in commercialism. I've always been a businessperson, but it's just that the way I do my business is different from most.[20] I like the concept of dressing people. I used to not care whether people bought the clothes or not, but I kind of like it now. I wouldn't label that commercialism; it's more like I do this work because I want people to wear it.[21]

What role do your clients play? Do you think
of them when you design your dresses?

When I'm working on a dress design I try to force myself to not go too far, because I always want my clients to understand what I'm doing. Even if I use my thirty minutes on the catwalk to express myself fully, I never lose sight of the fact that that particular item of clothing has to sell. If my clients don't grasp what I'm doing, I'm wasting my time.[22]

Are you bothered by the enormous sums
of money involved in fashion?

It's a completely different world, fashion, where I'm selling one of my dresses for 125 thousand pounds. It's like hello, that's a fucking castle in Scotland.[23]

I don't come from money, so I don't respect that kind of attitude. You know what it makes me feel like? It makes me feel like the movie *Seven*. You know when he's in the back of the car? I have the same kind of anger about money and people who gloat about it. There is no style in gloating about money. These silly cows who gloat about it in the press. It makes me quite sick. Decorum. That's the word.[24]

Given that you come from a working-class background,
what are your feelings about money?

I've got enough money to live on now but when I lose my passion for fashion then I quit. I've never been a very materialistic person so it's really hard to comprehend people who are because what are you going to do with it? I think I've always been the sort of person that'll end up poor at the end of it. I was born with shit, I'll fucking die with shit.[25]

What is the paradox of couture?

Couture shouldn't be approached from a business standpoint. There shouldn't be so much advertising. I find it sick, and grotesque. Couture has been turned into a business when in truth it's something entirely different. It's absurd and tragic to see that couture has lost its raison d'être, which is to be sublime. The sublime has turned into commercialism and advertising. It's lost its integrity.[26]

So the idea of a sublime dress — one that exalts the woman
wearing it — is very important to you?

I don't know what a sublime dress is until I design it. How to describe it? It comes naturally. It immediately jumps out at you. I tried to make dresses using pure gold, but it didn't work. You can attain the sublime using straw or some other base materials. The sublime can undoubtedly occur in fashion. The important thing is to never lose track of the goal, the quest.[27]

*Exactly, since you also want your work
to be accessible, and to sell.*

Couture is seen as a fad today, but I want mine to sell. Couture in the 1940s and 1950s actually sold to regular clients and I want to bring that back. I want to dress both the mothers and their daughters.[28]

Indeed, but customs have changed a lot since the 1950s.

I believe in the positive role of experience and evolution. Experience is never too heavy. Everything I've ever done has come out of a learning process; that's what allows me to move forward. But we don't let things evolve at their own pace. Fashion moves faster than the speed of light. When you talk of things evolving, you're talking about letting time do its thing. In the past, designers produced very few collections each year, and the changes they made were minute from one collection to another. For example, they would change the shape of the sleeves. These days I only have two days to come up with a whole new culture. The public wants more and more designs in a shorter and shorter amount of time, without realizing that this approach is killing fashion. We will no longer have transitions like those of the eighteenth to the twentieth centuries, when things evolved in such a way as to allow a revolution in form. Everything goes too fast. It's exhausting and terrifying. Time is cancer of the nerves.[29]

How would you describe your work?

There is always something sinister, something quite biographical about what I do — but that part is for me. It's my personal business. I think there is a lot of romance, melancholy. There's a sadness to it, but there's romance in sadness. I suppose I am a very melancholy person.[30] I may seem sad about my life and my work but I'm not bitter. I'm grateful for everything that's happened in my life.[31]

To what extent does your work reflect your life?

You can get insular with fashion. Sometimes I let you see what I am going through. It's biographical, but all my work is biographical in some sense. It has to be; otherwise there is no soul to it. . . It's good to know where you come from. It makes you what you are today. It's DNA, it's in your blood.[32]

Your ancestors weren't British.

No, they were French Huguenots who escaped across the channel during the French wars of religion.[33] My name is Scottish, and means "kin to the queen." At school, when I was a kid, people called me Queenie.[34]

Which is ironic, since you make no secret
of being opposed to the monarchy.

I'm anti-royalist. I don't believe in the royal family. I don't believe they do a job for the country; I just don't believe they are worth the money they are paid.[35] I don't believe in social classes. Why should we pay the royals to sit around and spend the public's money? However, I do believe that we create our own destiny. A poor person can make it through hard work.[36] The French Revolution tried to put an end to this hierarchy, but instead we ended up with a society that is even snobbier than before. Which pretty clearly reveals the true nature of human beings.[37]

And yet, in 2003 you received a CBE (Commander
of the Most Excellent Order of the British Empire)
from the hands of the queen.

Why they gave me that, I don't understand . . . I had this bloody hat with a feather in it, a big old bonnet, with a hangover. I'd been up at Annabel's and Claridge's all night; I was right frazzled. And my mum had me turning up in a Bentley. It was a funny day, but worth it. My mum loved it.[38]

You had promised yourself that you wouldn't look the
queen in the eye. But in the end you caved in.

I did. There was a simultaneous lock, and she started laughing,
and I started laughing . . . We caught it on camera where we're both
laughing at each other. She asked a question, "How long have you
been a fashion designer?" and I said, "A few years, m'lady." I wasn't
thinking straight — because I'd hardly had any sleep. I was really
tired. And I looked into her eyes, it was like when you see someone
across the room on a dance floor and you think, "Whoa." It was like
when I looked into her eyes, it was obvious that she had her fair
share of shit going on. I felt sorry for her. I've said a lot of stuff about
the queen in the past . . . but for that instant I had a bit of compassion
for her. So I came away feeling humbled by the situation.[39]

You continue to use her face in your work, if only symbolically.

The figure of the queen is present in all my collections — most
obviously in last summer's (spring/summer 2005), with the chess
set featuring lifelike white and black queens.[40]

You come from a large family.

I am the youngest of a family of six, and I grew up very close
to my three sisters. I feel that I experienced the positive and negative moments of their lives as women. They were very protective
of me. Women represent the calmer aspects of existence.[41] I hate
this thing about fragility and making women feel naive. I want
to empower women.[42] I saw how hard it was for mum to take care
of us. I try to promote and respect the strength of women.[43]

What kind of child were you? Well-behaved, or a little rascal?

They called me the bull, because I was always rushing headlong into
stuff, even though I was unsure of myself. When I was a kid I was lost.
I wasn't exactly violent, but I was feisty. When it was time to go for
it, I went for it. My thing was rugby. I loved getting tackled! I always
played forward; I loved the brutality of it.[44]

*Yet — and this is a particularly amusing detail —
you were also on the synchronized swimming team.*

I was the only boy out of forty girls. And my mum was so embarrassed, she couldn't watch me. I had to wear a grass skirt and go around in a circle.[45]

Do you see your parents regularly?

I'm still very close to my mum and dad . . . It's not easy. . . You look at their backgrounds. They were brought up in a part of East London called Stepney during World War II. My dad was beaten a lot by his father and his mother; my grandmother was a drunk. Beaten, so was the rest of his brothers and sisters, I mean, there was twelve of them. So you know, just trying to put food on the plate for twelve kids during wartime is not easy.[46]

*Nor is it easy in such a context to decide
to pursue an artistic profession.*

In a London working-class family, you have to bring home the bacon, and artistic routes are never seen as a means to that end. But I put my foot down . . . I thought, "I'm not gonna do that. I'm not gonna get married, live in a two-up, two-down and be a bloody black cab driver."[47] You know, I come from a very lower-class background. My father is a taxi driver; I have five siblings. At first, everybody was very worried about my career choice. Working-class people are very anxious about their sons, and tend to say, "Get a normal job, a real job." They ended up understanding that I was the "pink sheep" of the family. I've now been working for a dozen years or so. Most of my coworkers also come from working-class backgrounds. Our mothers have front-row seats at my shows. We look out for each other. I like that.[48]

How did you start out?

I was trained on Savile Row, in the workshops of the best English tailors. I started there at sixteen. That's how I was able to pay for my studies at the Saint Martin's School of Art. Which means that I know the cut of a suit or a dress. I am an able workman, a clothing craftsman — not an artist.[49]

What did you learn at the Saint Martin's School of Art?

How to be a fashion victim, and how to act like a designer! No, seriously — that's where I learned to bring together a collection, and develop a concept.[50] But you know, if you're good, it doesn't matter where you studied.[51]

Early on in your career you designed the infamous
"bumster" — low-rise pants that gave a peek of the top
of the cleft of the buttocks, a kind of backside cleavage.

It was an art thing, to change the way women looked, just by cut, to make a longer torso. But I was taking it to an extreme. The girls looked quite menacing, because there was so much top and so little bottom, because of the length of the legs.[52]

How would you describe your work?

My work has several facets to it, a hidden part and a visible one. And then one constant: all the women in my shows are powerful. They are in control of themselves and of the people around them.[53]

What do you have to offer to the men and
women who wear your designs?

I just try to make the person that's wearing them feel more confident in themselves because I am so unconfident. I'm really insecure in a lot of ways and I suppose my confidence comes out in the clothes I design anyway. I'm a very insecure person.[54]

In 1996 Bernard Arnault offered you the reins
of the Parisian house Givenchy. Do you remember
your first encounter with him?

He asked me, "Would you be interested in the Givenchy job?" And I just asked, "Where's the toilet?" I went to the toilet and sat there, mused. Then I came out and said I was interested.[55]

How do you truly feel about him?

He's both an angel and the devil, a businessman who can strike you down whenever he wants. When he approached me, I said yes out of a love of fashion. Money doesn't interest me — have you seen the clothes I wear! However, when he said he wanted to acquire a stake in my London company, I said no. Hubert de Givenchy's example was enough for me.[56]

*The least one can say is that your first collection
was not well-received by the press.*

Since we had no time, it was going to be a hit or miss, and it was a miss.[57]

Did you take it hard?

All those negative comments bothered me a lot, especially since
my words were often distorted. It wasn't even my idea to be put
in charge of this collection. And I never said I was going to
revolutionize an entire fashion house from one day to the next.[58]

*You were quoted as saying some very unfriendly
things about this esteemed institution.*

Some of the quotes attributed to me I never said. I don't want
to disrespect the gentleman who hired me, and whom I don't even
know. The thing is, I come from another generation, since I wasn't
even born yet in the 1950s. And I don't think it's disrespectful
to say that I don't have a 1960s vision of femininity.[59]

Any thoughts on fashion editors you'd care to share?

It's sad how little fashion editors really know about clothes.[60]
These people can make or break you, and they love you for just
a moment. I may be the name on everyone's lips at the moment,
but they can kill you.[61]

How did you initially perceive Givenchy?

Sexy and Parisian — the very things that were missing in French
fashion. Free of nostalgia, and the desire to do remakes.[62] Givenchy
made his name with clean tailoring, which came from his work with
Schiaparelli and his influence from Balenciaga. I want to bring back
that sophisticated wearability. . . more day suits and daywear for the
couture and certainly for the ready-to-wear.[63]

And your first impressions?

I've not done a bad job in bringing up the profile of a company people had only known for Audrey Hepburn... We all have to work towards a goal and we need to understand what that goal is. We need a consistent image, from the clothes to the advertising to the stores. I'm doing my best to make it work.[64]

Rumor has it that you attempted to leave before the end of your contract. Is that true?

Yeah, I did want to leave.[65] They said, "No, we can't let you leave," and I said, "Well in that case you're just going to let me do my fucking job." I will stick up for this house and say that I'm here and stay here till the end of my contract but I'm taking control of it from now on. Otherwise it's going to be the worst year of their lives.[66]
    You know the saying, "Too many cooks."[67] I still don't understand why they fucking hired me.[68] Basically, all these big companies don't care about you as a person. You're only a commodity and a product to them and only as good as your last collection.[69]

So what was your state of mind when you decided to continue?

Givenchy is a way for me to make money for my own company. It's not my conception of design, and there's no way I would apply it to McQueen. McQueen is my personal project. No one has the right to interfere in what I do.[70]

What is the major difference between your work at Givenchy and the designs you create for your own brand?

At the end of the day, Givenchy is 200 million light years away from what I do at McQueen. One is London, the other is Paris. It's two different aesthetics, and it's fucking hard to be both at the same time. McQueen is about our times, and Givenchy is about allure. They didn't employ me to do bumsters![71]

If people were expecting McQueen then they're stupid: I was giving them couture, which is about luxury and fantasy. People who wear that aren't interested in the real world. If you want a starving Ethiopian on a jacket then come to McQueen in London, if you want luxury, come to Givenchy. I'm a fashion schizophrenic.[72]

In 2001 French conglomerate Pinault-Printemps-Redoute (Kering) offered to finance your own brand.

As soon as you launch a self-named fashion house you turn into a businessman. My choice to work with PPR was dictated by the following considerations: they had the Bottega Veneta factories to make bags and the Sergio Rossi factories to make shoes — it's hard to do better than that. Though I'm part of the group, and obviously have a very sound management structure, I remain independent in my choices.[73]

How difficult is it to juggle the creative and business aspects of your work?

I think I'm very intelligent when it comes to my own company.[74] I'm mad in the front of my mind, but business-minded in the back.[75]

What does couture mean today?

It's synonymous with a certain cut. It's a kind of clothing fundamentalism. The thing that interests me is its architecture. The rest can fluctuate; it's just a question of details. Naturally, it's more difficult to create a well-cut jacket than to just put big bows everywhere. For me, nothing is more extravagant than to carry out an idea while demanding utmost quality. Before deconstructing fashion, the way it often is today, you have to know how to construct. Otherwise, you end up with nonsense.[76] Couture is not a jacket that has been so embroidered that it looks like someone vomited on it.[77] What's missing in French fashion is French chic. That means sexuality, allure, femininity, aloofness, and seductiveness, *mon chéri*. It's a nice curvy ass, a nice round bosom. And if you don't have any bosoms I'll put 'em there.[78]

*One often hears that Paris is no longer relevant in the
couture world. Do you agree with that assessment?*

Paris was the world capital of fashion, and never stopped gloating
about it. Paris needs to face up to its current difficulties. But it's not
a real fall from grace. Whatever one may think or say, Paris is very
good at marketing itself, and I find highly improbable that Paris
couture will disappear.[79]

*What kind of relationship do you have with the
workshops, and the men and women known
in French as "les petites mains"?*

I love them to death. I have a tremendous respect for their work and
experience and knowledge. That is what we need to protect, and use,
and cultivate . . . rather than obsolete dress styles or codes.[80] I myself
came out of a workshop, so I know that whenever you ask people
to work mechanically, they become aggressive. And it would really
be a shame not to use these fantastic talents.[81] You have to build up
a relationship based on trust with the people you are working with.
Any success is not just because of me. We've all made it the success
it is and the show of the season, because we know who we are.[82]

*While you were at Givenchy, you worked with some
of Parisian couture's most talented craftsmen and women.*

Before, I had never collaborated with the embroiderer Lesage, or with
the feather worker Lemarié. It takes a little time to find out what those
folks know how to do, and where their limits are, and it's only by
getting to know them better that I can keep moving forward.[83]

Do you have recurring influences?

Influences are really from my own imagination and not many
come from direct sources. They usually come from a lone force
of say, the way I want to perform sex or the way I want people to
perform sex or the way I want to see people act, or what would
happen if a person was like that . . . It's just sort of from a big
subconscious or the perverse.[84]

*You mentioned the Marquis de Sade as having
had an influence on your mindset.*

I gather some influence from the Marquis de Sade because I actually
think of him as a great philosopher and a man of his time, where
people found him just a pervert. [laughs] I find him sort of influential
in the way he provokes people's thoughts. It kind of scares me.[85]

*Between the design and marketing of your collections, the fashion
show is a key moment, and of utmost importance for you.*

I like blowing people's mind. It's a buzz. Like a fix, for twenty minutes.
I like the spontaneity of doing it there and then. We broke the mold by
not using the fashion-show-production people. I found Sam Gainsbury,
who'd been doing pop video. So it became more cinematic.[86] I use things
that people hide — war, religion, sex — and force them to look at them.[87]
I used to do it to shock people to provoke a reaction, but now I just do
it for myself. The shows always reflect where I am emotionally in my
own life.[88] With my shows you do get the feeling — the energy, buzz
and excitement — you'd get in a rock concert.[89] Fashion should be a form
of escapism, and not a form of imprisonment.[90]

How do you feel about the idea of an emotional journey?

I like emotion. I've got nothing against people crying at my shows. I try
to push the limits of fashion. I like to imagine Amazons — independent,
almost tribal-looking women. As different as you could imagine from
people today, who are often controlled and constrained by outside forces.[91]

Does one show stick out in your mind?

It was my best show [spring/summer 1999], that moment with Shalom
[Harlow]! That combination of arts and crafts with technology — that
weird unison between man and machine. I remember doing the tests
with Katy England before. The insurance was a million pounds that
day — a stupid amount! We got the machines from Fiat in Italy,
where they're used for painting cars. And now they've ripped it off
in a TV commercial, haven't they? You find a lot of ideas from my
shows in adverts now. I find it a compliment.[92]

There was also the "asylum" show (spring/summer 2001), where journalists found themselves seated around an enormous Perspex box that reflected their image, until it was lit from within, marking the start of the show.

Ha! I was really pleased about that. I was looking at it on the monitor, watching everyone trying not to look at themselves. It was a great thing to do in the fashion industry — turn it back on them! God, I've done some freaky shows.[93]

Instead of opting for elaborate ad campaigns, you like theatrical fashion shows that generate publicity in and of themselves.

I don't go in for ad campaigns because the thing I like in photography is the "instant," the "moment," to quote Cartier-Bresson, and I'm not sure I would be able to obtain that kind of result with another photographer. So what's the point of spending money for a result that I won't be fully satisfied with? On the other hand, I have the impression that I'm expressing myself fully in my fashion shows, which are a vehicle for my fantasies. I spent years devising the hologram of Kate Moss that appeared at the end of my 2006 show. It was a great technical achievement . . . And in the end, by creating these intensely emotional moments, I get more media coverage than if I had had a regular ad campaign.[94]

What designers do you admire?

The people I respect, such as Martin Margiela and Rei Kawakubo (from Comme des Garçons) are able to rip apart and remake an article of clothing. Even if they remake it in an entirely different way, it's still an exercise in virtuosity, and elegance. That's where you find the greatest eccentricity.[95] Today we're thinking faster than Rei. You have no choice.[96]

And among French designers?

Well, of course I deeply admire Monsieur Saint Laurent. When we were students, he was the absolute reference. I'm sure he was exactly like us when he was young. Naturally, things have changed . . . I prefer to ignore his comments about me.[97]

What is the role of contemporary fashion designers?

You can't depend on fashion designers to predict the future of society, you know, at the end of the day they're only clothes and that never strays from my mind for one minute.[98]

These days you hear people talk more about fashion brands than about actual designers.

You know what killed fashion off? Those fucking logos, they brought it down to the level of advertising.[99]

Should fashion be provocative?

Absolutely. That's the goal. Fashion should get reactions from people; that's what I strive to do. For example, when you get dressed for a job interview, you want to be the best you can be, and project a sensual, sexually charged image. When you try to get a reaction, people see your personality in a totally different light.[100]

What is it like to be constantly searching for the new?

The new doesn't exist. Even in the most contemporary design. If you look closely we haven't evolved that much from ancient Egyptian cups. Nothing is new under the sun. Materials evolve, fabrics change . . . But, even if themes are different, everything is part of the same whole. The idea is to use material to transform a human body. Within this eternal return, I can only believe in my own evolution. But you can never escape the past. We are anchored to it and it's crucial — especially nowadays when everything is going faster and faster. Technology is gaining ground on human nature. Or rather, human nature now has to transcend technology. The cut of the clothes has to be shot through with human feeling. That's what links us to History and time past.[101] My sensitivity makes me scuttle back and forth between life and death, happiness and sadness, good and evil. And indeed, all of that is one and the same. It comes out of life, and experience. When I look at the work of Titian or Caravaggio, I feel the same thing. Or from the artists whose work I collect, such as Sam Taylor-Wood, Joel-Peter Witkin, and Andres Serrano.[102]

Could you describe your creative process?

I have to be true to myself and if the creative process takes me away from the original brief, then I have to be brave, take the risk, and be prepared to stand by it.[103]

What makes things fall into place?

Pattern codes and proportions are my starting point.[104] The cut is really all about, and accentuates, what I personally find attractive and sexy.[105] Fabrics are so important that I wait till the last minute to select them.[106]

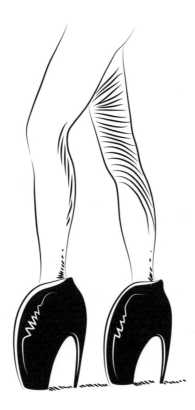

*In an increasingly competitive industry in which time
is more often than not the enemy, how do you find the
strength to keep moving forward?*

Time is *the* raw material. However, it's personal, emotional time.
My clothes aren't so much about the seasons as about the times
I live in, and the moment. All of my designs come out of the emotions
I am feeling at that given moment. The seasons themselves are
conceptual, and out of sync, since I design "winter" in summer,
and vice versa. For me, winter is linked to melancholy, while summer
is a break in the rush, a pause . . . I try, within my designs, to accentuate the "happy" times. I think that contemporary fashion should
be liberating, and that we need to forge our present through it.
That being said, sometimes there is a contrast between the public's
expectations and my personal feelings. I suppose that my "moods,"
which can at times seem odd, come out of the conflict between
my own emotions and what I have to do for the public.[107]

*Your muse, friend, and very first patron, Isabella Blow
committed suicide in 2007. Your spring/summer 2008
collection is an homage to her.*

Before Issie's death, I was already going through a transition in
my life. I was asking myself deep questions, such as: Should I really
continue doing this job when I really don't like fashion and dislike
the people involved in it? Then, more recently, the parameters began
to change, and there was that collection, that I got behind one
hundred percent — going so far as to cut some of the patterns myself.
Strangely enough, I rediscovered that that is what I really like to do.
I also realized that the end result of the work consists in making
clothes for people, and that you can do that without necessarily
making commercial compromises.[108]

*Do you enjoy being famous? Is being famous
a kind of revenge on your past?*

I've always been a wallflower, I like to look in on the situation
but it's really brain-fucky 'cause all of a sudden the wall's turned
right around on you. And I don't like it. It's really freaked me out.
I can feel it now that I'm a more famous person and it gives me
panic attacks. I'm even shaking right now thinking about it.[109]
　　　I'm a fashion designer, not a movie actor or pop star.
The problem today with celebrity is that everything becomes
so personal: you have to exhibit your "lifestyle." I don't want
to do that. The only thing I ask myself is how to keep my business
successful while remaining true to myself. I follow my own path,
and in my own sweet time. Without any desire whatsoever to see
my clothes in all the supermarkets.[110]

*If you were going to invite a famous historical
figure to dinner, who would it be?*

Jesus of Nazareth, to check if he really exists, and it's not just
we've been reading some Peter Pan book for the past 2,000 years.
Or Mel Gibson to be there if Jesus wasn't true.[111]

*Is there a historical period whose aesthetic
is particularly congenial to you?*

I'm thinking! Fifteenth-century Flemish, Netherlands. My favorite
part of art. Because of the colors, because of the sympathetic way
they approached life... Cause I think they were very modern for
their times, in that period and in that part of the world.[112]

*You began working at sixteen; now you've been at it for
almost twenty-five years. How different do you feel?*

You get complacent. Sometimes I see myself get that way... I get very
confused about fashion to the point that I'm not interested in it.
There isn't that spontaneity where the aesthetic comes from within...
When I was doing what I thought [was] fantastic work, I didn't give
a shit what people thought.[113]

What kind of life do you want your designs to lead?
How would you like them to be perceived through time?

I'm interested in designing for posterity. People who buy McQueen are going to hand the clothes down to their children, and that's very rare today.[114]

Do you feel misunderstood?

What people think is aggression is passion for what I believe.[115] I'm not tortured; I'm schizophrenic. I express the collision of my contradictions: romanticism encased in sadomasochism, for example.[116] I'm actually a nice guy.[117]

What bothers you the most about the fashion world?

The superficiality of it escapes me totally . . . Just because you're talented for art, fashion, or music doesn't mean that you need to be rude or to act superior to other people. It comes back to smack you in the face one day. The worst thing about Kate Moss was the disgusting climate of hypocrisy surrounding her. Everybody in this milieu is putting dope up their noses. Personally, I've always had a very frank attitude. Which made me a lot of enemies. Some people would rather not work with me at all because they're afraid of my outspokenness.[118]

Are drugs inherent to fashion and its stressful environment?

This job is a drug in itself, and drugs are part of the job. Fashion is "the number one killer." You have to control everything, from the scoring and ingesting to the setting up of meetings.[119]

And how about you?

Yeah. I do drugs. Yeah, I've experienced everything there is to experience. Don't tell me there's anyone in my business who hasn't.[120]

What is the personality flaw that exasperates you the most?

Bigotry.[121]

What keeps you going?

It's the insecurity that drives me.[122] Self-satisfaction is the failing I fear most. Many people in this business fall into that. You end up believing all the compliments that people shower you with. You begin to take it for granted, and that's when everything goes awry. You can never take anything for granted in fashion. The only way to keep going in the right direction is to be constantly apprehensive. Fear is my best friend.[123]

Your passion for birds is well known.
Why are birds so important to you?

My approach to birds is similar to Leonardo da Vinci's. He wanted human beings to be able to fly, and expressed that desire through his artistic, architectural, but also his scientific sensibility. Birds in flight fascinate me. I admire eagles and falcons. When I look at a feather, I get inspiration from its color, its design, its lightness, its engineering. It's such an intricate thing. In truth, my work is an attempt to make women as beautiful as birds.[124]

With all this coming and going to and fro from London
and Paris, have you learned to speak French?

I speak with my hands. I have golden hands. Just call me Goldfinger.[125]

⸻ NOTES ⸺

1   Pascale Renaux, "Face à face: Apocalypse Now!" *Numéro*, December 2000/January 2001, 39.

2   Bridget Foley, "The Alexander Method," *WWD*, August 31, 1999.

3   Foley, "The Alexander Method."

4   Marie-Pierre Lannelongue, "Save McQueen," *Elle*, February 12, 2007, 71–72.

5   Renaux, "Face à face: Apocalypse now!" 43.

6   Mark C. O'Flaherty, "Alexander McQueen," *The Pink Paper*, May 12, 1994, markcoflaherty.wordpress.com/tag/alexander-mcqueens-first-interview.

7   Dana Thomas, "The King of Shock," *Newsweek*, March 17, 1997, 44.

8   Tim Blanks, "The Tragedy of McQueen," *Vogue* (UK), May 2010, 166.

9   Tim Blanks, "Long Live McQueen," *ES Fashion*, September 2004, 100.

10 Blanks, "The Tragedy of McQueen," 170.

11 James Fallon, "McQueen: He'll Do It His Way," *WWD*, October 15, 1996.

12 Renaux, "Face à face: Apocalypse now!" 40.

13 Foley, "The Alexander Method."

14 Jessica Kerwin, "London's 'Wild Child' Visits New York," *WWD*, September 13, 1999.

15 Foley, "The Alexander Method."

16 Lannelongue, "Save McQueen," 76.

17 Cécile Sepulchre, "Alexander McQueen veut que les femmes aient 'l'air invincible,'" *Journal du Textile*, March 10, 1997, 47.

18 "David Bowie vs Alexander McQueen," *Dazed & Confused*. Issue 26, November 1996.

19 O'Flaherty, "Alexander McQueen."

20 Foley, "The Alexander Method."

21 Susannah Frankel, "The Real McQueen," *Harper's Bazaar*, April 1, 2007.

22 Sepulchre, "Alexander McQueen veut que les femmes aient 'l'air invincible,'" 48.

23 Simon Gage, "Alexander McQueen," *Arena*, December 2000, 100.

24 Kate Betts, "McCabre McQueen" *Vogue*, October 1997, 385.

25 Gage, "Alexander McQueen," 98.

26 Virginie Luc, "Alexander McQueen: Le temps est un tueur," *Vogue* (France), October 2010, 288.

27 Luc, "Alexander McQueen: Le temps est un tueur."

28 Fallon, "McQueen: He'll Do It His Way."

29 Luc, "Alexander McQueen: Le temps est un tueur."

30 Sarah Mower, "McQueen, The Showman," Style.com, February 13, 2010.

31 Blanks, "The Tragedy of McQueen," 166.

32 Godfrey Deeny, "Alexander McQueen: The Final Interview," *Harper's Bazaar*, March 8, 2010.

33 François Baudot, "Je ne suis pas agressif, je suis un pussy cat," *Elle* (France), March 9, 1998, 165.

34 Anne Boulay, "Reine de cœur," *Vogue* (France), October 2005, 230.

35 Gage, "Alexander McQueen," 98.

36 Sepulchre, "Alexander McQueen veut que les femmes aient 'l'air invincible,'" 47.

37 Sepulchre, "Alexander McQueen veut que les femmes aient 'l'air invincible,'" 47.

38 Mower, "McQueen, The Showman."

39 Joyce McQueen, "Alexander McQueen Interviewed . . . By His Mum," *The Guardian*, April 20, 2004, theguardian.com/culture/2004/apr/20/guesteditors.

40 Boulay, "Reine de cœur," 230.

41 Boulay, "Reine de cœur," 230.

42 Betts, "McCabre McQueen," 435.

43 Thomas, "The King of Shock," 44.

44 Philippe Trétiak, "Alexander McQueen un hooligan chez Givenchy," *Elle* (France), "Il" supplement, April 21, 1997, 52.

45 Foley, "The Alexander Method."

46 Foley, "The Alexander Method."

47 Foley, "The Alexander Method."

48 Baudot, "Je ne suis pas agressif, je suis un pussy cat," 170.

49 Baudot, "Je ne suis pas agressif, je suis un pussy cat," 170.

50 Paquita Paquin, "Alexander McQueen," *Dépêche Mode*, March 1997, 99.

51 Sepulchre, "Alexander McQueen veut que les femmes aient 'l'air invincible,'" 47.

52 Mower, "McQueen, The Showman."

53 Boulay, "Reine de cœur," 230.

54 "David Bowie vs Alexander McQueen."

55 David Kamp, "London Swings! Again!" *Vanity Fair*, March 1997.

56 Janie Samet, "Chez Givenchy: God Save Mac Queen," *Le Figaro*, January 16, 1997.

57 Betts, "McCabre McQueen," 385.

58 Sepulchre, "Alexander McQueen veut que les femmes aient 'l'air invincible,'" 47.

59 Sepulchre, "Alexander McQueen veut que les femmes aient 'l'air invincible,'" 47.

60 Betts, "McCabre McQueen," 384.

61 O'Flaherty, "Alexander McQueen."

62 Samet, "Chez Givenchy: God Save Mac Queen."

63 Fallon, "McQueen: He'll Do It His Way."

64 Bridget Foleyn, "King McQueen," *W magazine,* September 1999, 458.

65 Avril Mair, "McQueen Meets Knight," *I-D*, July 2000, 89.

66 Gage, "Alexander McQueen," 96.

67 Gage, "Alexander McQueen," 96.

68 Mair, "McQueen Meets Knight," 89.

69 Miles Socha, "McQueen's Future: Will He Say Adieu to House Givenchy?" *WWD*, September 13, 2000.

70 Renaux, "Face à face: Apocalypse now!" 40.

71 Plum Sykes, "Couture Kid," *Vogue* (UK), April 1997, 164.

72 Sykes, "Couture Kid," 234.

73 Lannelongue, "Save McQueen," 76.

74 Socha, "McQueen's Future: Will He Say Adieu to House Givenchy?"

75 "Alexander McQueen, A True Master" *WWD*, February 12, 2010, 7.

76 Baudot, "Je ne suis pas agressif, je suis un pussy cat," 170.

77 François Reynaert, "Givenchy le terrible," *Le Nouvel Observateur*, January 30, 1997.

78 Sykes, "Couture Kid," 164.

79 Sepulchre, "Alexander McQueen veut que les femmes aient l'air invincible," 49.

80 Baudot, "Je ne suis pas agressif, je suis un pussy cat," 170.

81 Sepulchre, "Alexander McQueen veut que les femmes aient l'air invincible," 47.

82 Frankel, "The Real McQueen."

83 Paquin, "Alexander McQueen," 98.

84 "David Bowie vs Alexander McQueen."

85 "David Bowie vs Alexander McQueen."

86 Mower, "McQueen, The Showman."

87 Véronique Lorelle, "Alexander McQueen," *Le Monde*, February 13, 2010.

88 Frankel, "The Real McQueen."

89 Hamish Bowles, "Avant-garde Designer of the Year Alexander McQueen," *Vogue*, December 1999, 154.

90 Miles Socha, "The Great Escape," *WWD*, April 13, 2009, 62.

91 Lannelongue, "Save McQueen," 72–74.

92 Mower, "McQueen, The Showman."

93 Mower, "McQueen, The Showman."

94 Lannelongue, "Save McQueen," 72.

95 Baudot, "Je ne suis pas agressif, je suis un pussy cat," 170.

96 Cathy Horyn, "General Lee," *New York Times Style Magazine*, September 26, 2009, 67.

97 Baudot, "Je ne suis pas agressif, je suis un pussy cat," 169.

98 "David Bowie vs Alexander McQueen."

99 Blanks, "Long Live McQueen," 98.

100 Paquin, "Alexander McQueen," 99.

101 Luc, "Alexander McQueen: Le temps est un tueur," 288.

102 Pascale Renaux, "Angel heart," *Numéro*, December 2007/January 2008, 222.

103 Isaac Lock, "Fashion in Flight," *Dazed & Confused*, November 2009, 121.

104 O'Flaherty, "Alexander McQueen."

105 Horyn, "General Lee," 67.

106 Sepulchre, "Alexander McQueen veut que les femmes aient l'air invincible," 48.

107 Luc, "Alexander McQueen: Le temps est un tueur," 288.

108 Renaux, "Angel heart," 222.

109 Gage, "Alexander McQueen," 98.

110 Lannelongue, "Save McQueen," 76.

111 McQueen, "Alexander McQueen Interviewed . . . By His Mum."

112 McQueen, "Alexander McQueen Interviewed . . . By His Mum."

113 Mair, "McQueen Meets Knight," 89.

114 "Alexander McQueen: In his own words" Harpersbazaar.com, February 11, 2010.

115 Foley, "The Alexander Method."

116 Géraldine de Margerie, "Alexander McQueen (1969–2010)," *Les Inrockuptibles*, February 17, 2010, 20.

117 Foley, "The Alexander Method."

118 Renaux, "Angel heart," 220.

119 Trétiak, "Alexander McQueen un hooligan chez Givenchy," 52.

120 Gage, "Alexander McQueen," 102.

121 McQueen, "Alexander McQueen Interviewed . . . By His Mum."

122 Sykes, "Couture Kid," 164.

123 Baudot, "Je ne suis pas agressif, je suis un pussy cat," 170.

124 Renaux, "Angel Heart," xiv.

125 Samet, "Chez Givenchy: God Save Mac Queen."

WHAT IS FASHION?

A ROUND TABLE DISCUSSION

By way of concluding, I propose a round table discussion in the intimate company of our panel of experts exploring the question on everyone's mind: What is fashion?

Mademoiselle Chanel, shall we begin with you?

What is fashion? You tell me. I am certain that not one single soul would be able to give a valid answer . . . And I include myself.[1]

And how about you, Madame Grès?

For me, fashion does not exist; I create things that I find pleasing. That is all.[2]

What does our doyenne, Madame Lanvin, have to say on the matter?

Couture is not an abstract art.[3]

Monsieur Saint Laurent, might we trouble you for a comment?

I don't consider what I do to be fashion! Women who follow fashion are following an event — they want to discover the new gadget. As for me, I don't participate in the "spectacle" of fashion.[4]

Et tu, Alexander McQueen?

Fashion isn't much, just clothes. The important thing is to bring to life one's ideas.[5]

Madame Schiaparelli, you look as if you are eager to interject.

Dare to be different.[6]

Monsieur Dior, could you give us an inkling
of your position on this matter?

Even the most uninformed person can see the painstaking effort
that has gone into the maddest collections. The great adventure
of Paris fashion design is not merely a sort of Vanity Fair. It is the
outward sign of an ancient civilization, which intends to survive.[7]
Fashion, in this age of machines, has become one of the last
refuges of the human, personal, and individual element.[8]

Pierre Balmain, and you?

There are many trends, but fashion is what endures.[9]

You were saying, Madame Vionnet?

The end goal of our métier is to create dresses that combine
a harmonious body and a pleasantly proportioned silhouette,
to create beauty. That's what it's all about![10]

Monsieur Poiret, as our resident king of fashion,
I will let you have the last word.

Believe me, fashion is like rain or phylloxera, you have to wait for
it to end . . . And by definition pass it must. One must consider
fashion like an old relative who is a bit dotty. Her strange ideas
shouldn't be held against her, since we know she's not thinking
straight, and soon this, too, shall pass.[11]

(True to form, Cristóbal Balenciaga does not utter a single word.)

Thank you to everyone.

⸺◖ NOTES ◗⸻

1 Coco Chanel, "La mode, Qu'est
que c'est?" On side 2 of sound recording
Coco Chanel Parle. Hugues Desalle.

2 Chantal Zerbib, "'La femme n'est
pas un clown' ou la mode vue par
Madame Grès," *Lire*, May 1984, 84.

3 Jeanne Lanvin, "Le Cinéma influence-t-il
la Mode?" *Le Figaro Illustré*,
February 1933, 78.

4 Hélène de Turckheim, "Saint Laurent
dessine son 'été 34' et répond aux
questions," *Le Figaro*, October 16, 1973.

5 Philippe Tretiak, "Alexander McQueen
un hooligan chez Givenchy," *Elle* (France),
"Il" supplement, April 21, 1997.

6 Ormond Gigli, "A Woman Chic,"
The Los Angeles Times, May 8, 1955, K9.

7 Christian Dior, *Christian Dior
and I*, trans. Antonia Fraser
(New York: Dutton, 1957), 236.

8 Christian Dior, *Talking About Fashion*,
trans. Eugenia Sheppard (New York:
Putnam, 1954), 55.

9 "À la mode de chez nous," "Une conférence
pas comme les autres de Pierre Balmain"
(sous l'égide du Cercle Interallié), 1984,
manuscript, Centre de Documentation
Mode, Musée des Arts Décoratifs, Paris.

10 Gaston Derys, "En devisant avec . . .
Madeleine Vionnet," Minerva, illustrated
supplement to the Journal de Rouen,
January 2, 1938, 7.

11 Paul Poiret, "La Mode et la Mort,"
Les Arts Décoratifs Modernes, 1925, 63.

LIST OF ILLUSTRATIONS

SELECTED BIBLIOGRAPHY

Ballard, Bettina. *In My Fashion*. New York: Secker & Warburg, 1960.

Beaton, Cecil. *The Glass of Fashion*. New York: Doubleday, 1954.

———. *Memoirs of the 40s*. New York: McGraw-Hill Book Company, 1972.

Benaïm, Laurence. *Yves Saint Laurent*. Paris: Éditions Grasset, 2002.

Blum, Dilys. *Shocking! The Art and Fashion of Schiaparelli*. Philadelphia, PA: Philadelphia Museum of Art, 2003.

Blume, Mary, *The Master of Us All : Balenciaga, His Workrooms, His World*. New York: Farrar, Straus and Giroux, 2013.

Bolton, Andrew. *Alexander McQueen, Savage Beauty*. New York: The Metropolitan Museum of Art, 2011.

Charles-Roux, Edmond. *Chanel and Her World*. New York: Vendome Press, 2005.

Chase, Edna Woolman, and Ilka Chase, *Always in Vogue*. London: Victor Gollancz Ltd., 1954.

Christian Dior, Hommage à Christian Dior 1947–1957. Paris, Musée des Arts de la Mode, 1987.

Dior, Christian. *Talking about Fashion*. Translated by Eugenia Sheppard. New York: Putnam, 1954.

———. *Christian Dior and I*. Translated by Antonia Fraser. New York: Dutton, 1957.

———. *Conférences écrites par Christian Dior pour la Sorbonne, 1955–1957*. Paris: Éditions du Regard / Institut Français de la Mode, 2003.

Drake, Alicia. *The Beautiful Fall: Lagerfeld, Saint Laurent, and Glorious Excess in 1970s Paris*. New York: Little, Brown and Company, 2006.

Fairchild, John. *The Fashionable Savages*. New York: Doubleday, 1965.

Golbin, Pamela. *Fashion Designers*. New York: Watson-Guptill Publications, 2000.

Golbin, Pamela, ed. *Balenciaga Paris*. London: Thames & Hudson Ltd., 2006.

———. *Madeleine Vionnet*. New York: Rizzoli International Publications, 2009.

Grumbach, Didier. *History of International Fashion*. New York: Interlink Publishing, 2014.

Jeanne Lanvin. Paris: Paris Musées, 2015.

Pochna, Marie-France. *Christian Dior*. Introduction by John Galliano. New York: The Overlook Press, 2009.

Poiret, Paul, *En Habillant l'Epoque*. Paris: Éditions Grasset, 1930.

———. *Revenez-y*. Paris: Éditions Gallimard, 1932.

Saint Laurent, Yves. *Yves Saint Laurent*. New York: The Metropolitan Museum of Art, 1983.

Schiaparelli, Elsa. *Shocking Life*. London: J. M. Dent & Sons, 1954.

Snow, Carmel, with Mary Louise Aswell. *The World of Carmel Snow*. New York: McGraw-Hill, 1962.

Vreeland, Diana. *D.V.* Edited by George Plimpton and Christopher Hemphill. New York: Alfred A. Knopf, 1984.

———. "Balenciaga: An Appreciation." In *The World of Balenciaga*. New York: The Metropolitan Museum of Art, 1973.

Warhol, Andy. *The Philosophy of Andy Warhol (From A to B and Back Again)*. New York: Harcourt Books, 1975.

Yves Saint Laurent par Yves Saint Laurent. Paris: Herscher / Musée des Arts de la Mode, 1986.

BIOGRAPHIES

Cristóbal **Balenciaga** was born on January 21, 1895, in Getaria (Basque Country of Spain) and died on March 24, 1972, in Jávea, Spain, at the age of seventy-seven. He founded his Parisian house in 1937, then, in 1968, retired and closed its doors.

Pierre **Balmain** was born on May 18, 1914, in Saint-Jean-de-Maurienne, France, and died in Paris on June 29, 1982, at the age of sixty-eight. After working with Christian Dior at the house of Lucien Lelong, he opened his own house in 1945. He would sell it in 1970 but would continue to design there until his death.

Gabrielle Bonheur **Chanel** was born on August 19, 1883, in Saumur, France. She died in Paris on January 10, 1971, at the age of eighty-eight. The house of Chanel opened in 1912 and would close its doors in 1939, on the eve of World War II. In 1953, at the age of seventy, Chanel reopened her house.

Christian **Dior** was born on January 21, 1905, in Granville, France, and would die on October 24, 1957, in Montecatini, Italy, at the age of fifty-two. He created his own house of couture at a late stage, in 1946. Yves Saint Laurent, who joined the house in 1955, succeeded him after his death.

Jacques **Doucet** was born in Paris on February 19, 1853. He died in Neuilly-sur-Seine on October 30, 1929, at the age of seventy-six. The Doucet house of lingerie, founded by his parents in 1816, prospered under his leadership and became one of the premier houses of haute couture in Paris, where he trained Paul Poiret and Madeleine Vionnet.

Germaine Émilie Krebs, known as Madame **Grès**, was born in Paris on November 30, 1903, and died on November 24, 1993, at the age of ninety. She began her career under the name Alix, then opened the house of Grès in 1941. In 1984 it was bought out by the French businessman Bernard Tapie.

Jeanne-Marie **Lanvin**, born in Paris on January 1, 1867, died in Paris on July 6, 1946, at the age of seventy-nine. She opened a millinery shop under her name in 1885, developed it into a couture house, and would continue to work until her death. It is to this day the oldest such house in continuous operation.

Lucien **Lelong**, born in Paris on October 11, 1889, died in Anglet, France, on May 11, 1958, at the age of sixty-nine. He ran the house of couture created by his parents, which had as many as twelve hundred employees. It would close in 1948. He also trained Pierre Balmain and Christian Dior. Thanks to his authority as President of the Chambre Syndicale de la Haute Couture, during World War II Parisian couture was not transplanted to Berlin under control of the Nazis.

Alexander **McQueen**, born in London on March 17, 1969, died in London on February 11, 2010, having committed suicide at the age of forty-one. McQueen designed under his own name beginning in 1992 and up to his death, producing thirty-six collections. In addition, between October 1996 and March 2001 McQueen designed the haute couture and prêt-à-porter collections for the house of Givenchy.

Edward **Molyneux**, known as Captain Molyneux, was born in London on September 5, 1891, and died in Monte Carlo on March 23, 1974, at the age of eighty-three. He opened his first house in Paris in 1919 and would retire in 1969. He is credited with designing the wedding gown worn by Wallis Simpson in 1937 for her marriage to Prince Edward, Duke of Windsor.

Paul Robert **Piguet** was born in Yverdon-les-Bains, Switzerland, on May 6, 1898, and died in Lausanne, Switzerland, on February 21, 1953, at the age of fifty-five. He débuted under his own name in 1920, then worked at the house of Poiret before successfully reopening his house. It closed in 1951. He hired in succession Christian Dior and Hubert de Givenchy.

Paul-Henri **Poiret** was born in Paris on April 20, 1879. He would die in Paris on April 30, 1944, at the age of sixty-five. He opened his house of couture in September 1903 and closed it in 1929, during the economic crisis brought on by the stock market crash.

Yves Mathieu-**Saint-Laurent** was born on August 1, 1936, in Oran, Algeria, and died in Paris on June 1, 2008, at the age of seventy-two. His couture house opened in 1961. At a press conference on January 7, 2002, Yves Saint Laurent announced his retirement.

Elsa **Schiaparelli**, born in Rome on September 10, 1890, died in 1973 on November 13, at the age of eighty-three. She founded her house in Paris in 1927 and would close it in 1954 as a result of financial difficulties.

Marie Madeleine Valentine **Vionnet** was born in Chilleurs-aux-Bois, France, on June 22, 1876. She died in Paris on March 2, 1975, at the age of ninety-nine. She struck out on her own in 1912. When World War II broke out, she decided to close her house definitely.

Charles-Frederick **Worth** was born in England on October 13, 1825, and died in 1895 on March 10, at the age of seventy. He founded his own house in 1857. He was the first to have living models show his collection, developed the concept of seasonal collections, and above all invented the figure of the celebrity fashion designer that still prevails today.

AUTHOR BIOGRAPHIES

Pamela **Golbin** is Chief Curator of Fashion and Textiles at the Musée des Arts Décoratifs in Paris. She has organized over twenty exhibitions and authored their catalogues, including major retrospectives on iconic fashion designers such as *Balenciaga Paris* (2006), *Madeleine Vionnet* (2009), *Hussein Chalayan* (2011), *Louis Vuitton / Marc Jacobs* (2012), and *Dries Van Noten* (2013). Ms. Golbin initiated the annual Fashion Talks interviews in New York City, bringing onto a public stage the most renowned names in contemporary fashion for one-on-one live discussion. She is also a frequent commentator on television and radio in Europe and abroad. To celebrate the thirty-year anniversary of the national costumes collections at the Musée des Arts Décoratfis, she curated the exhibition *Fashion Forward: Three Centuries of Fashion*, a survey of the history of fashion at the museum from the eighteenth century to the present day (2016).

Hamish **Bowles**, International Editor at Large for *Vogue*, is recognized as one of the most respected authorities of fashion and interior design. In addition to collecting and amassing an extensive private collection of historic haute couture, Mr. Bowles has curated numerous exhibitions, including *Jacqueline Kennedy: The White House Years* (2001); *Balenciaga: Spanish Master* (2010); and *Balenciaga and Spain* (2011), and has also written countless articles, reviews, and books, including: *Vogue: The Covers* (2011); *Vogue: The Editor's Eye* (2012); *Vogue Weddings: Brides, Dresses, Designers* (2012); and *Vogue and The Metropolitan Museum of Art Costume Institute: Parties, Exhibitions, & People* (2014).

Yann **Legendre**'s illustrations have appeared in more than fifty publications, including the *Wall Street Journal* and the *New York Times*. Previous books include *Grimm's Fairy Tales* (Rockport, 2014). He is a member of the Society of Illustrators in New York.

ACKNOWLEDGMENTS

I wish to express my sincere gratitude to
Anthony Petrillose, Antoinette d'Aboville, Charles Miers,
Catherine Bonifassi, Delphine Saurat, Dung Ngo, Emmanuelle Beuvin,
Giulia Di Filippo, Hamish Bowles, Jacob Wildschiødtz,
Jerome Gautier, Joan Juliet Buck, Johny G, Madeleine Chapsal,
Matthew Appleton, Odile Premel, Philippe Aronson,
Sheila Sitaram, and Yann Legendre.

I dedicate this book to my one and only JFL

To LBG
To Mathilde, Stefan, August, and Matias
To P

And to X!

No sooner has one fashion destroyed another than it is wiped out in turn by a newcomer that will yield to the next, which will not be the last: such is our frivolity.

— Jean de la Bruyère
Les Caractères ou les Moeurs de ce siècle, 1687

Paul Poiret.

Jacques Fath

M. Piguet

Gabrielle Chanel

Elsa Schiaparelli

Cristóbal Balenciaga

Christian Dior

Alix Grès.

Pierre Balmain

Yves Saint Laurent